CHRISSY FREER is a nutritionist and food writer who has developed a signature style of delicious recipes with a holistic health focus. She has published two books with Murdoch Books, *supergrains* and *superlegumes*, and writes for a range of magazines and websites. Her recipes use whole, unprocessed foods to provide balanced nutrition and include low-GI, gluten-free and dairy-free options.

Chrissy lives in the beautiful Byron Bay region with her daughter, Harriet, and loves using the area's abundant local produce in her recipe development and cooking.

www.chrissyfreer.com

REAL
DELICIOUS

✦✦✦

CHRISSY
FREER

REAL
DELICIOUS

✦✦✦

100+ WHOLEFOOD
RECIPES FOR HEALTH
AND WELLNESS

MURDOCH BOOKS

SYDNEY · LONDON

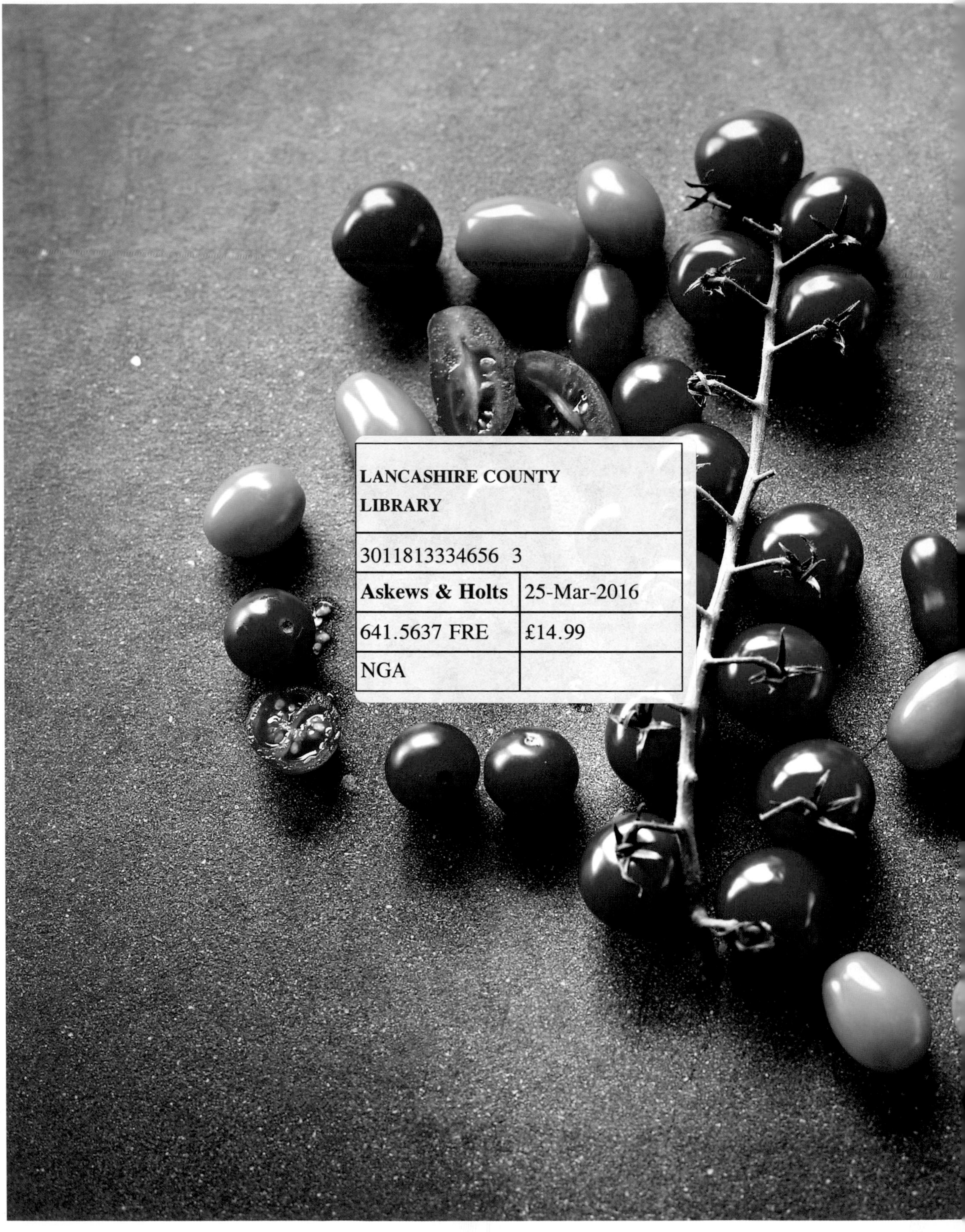

CONTENTS

MORE CHOICE, LESS WELLBEING?

Once upon a time, choosing what to eat was easy: our ancestors hungrily devoured whatever they could find, forage, hunt or grow. But times have changed and most of us now have the luxury of living with an abundance of food. This immense choice brings its own challenges.

Whether it's the result of persuasive advertising, the huge variety of products on the supermarket shelves, or the constant, ever-changing and ever-contradictory flow of dietary advice on the internet and in magazines, choosing what to eat for good health and enjoyment has never felt so complicated. Even as a nutritionist I sometimes find the choice overwhelming. Navigating the vast amounts of information and mass of choices that is the food industry in the twenty-first century can be a pretty tricky business.

SO, WHY DO WE EAT?

Our bodies need energy to function, our brains need energy to keep us alive, and we get this energy from food. Everything we eat can be broken down into two basic categories: macronutrients and micronutrients.

Macronutrients are the main nutrient groups: protein, carbohydrate and fat. It's these that provide us with the energy required for growth and living. An easy way to remember is that macro means 'large' – and we need these nutrients in large quantities.

Micronutrients are our vitamins and minerals. They don't provide us with energy (kilojoules), but they are essential for good health, for growth and for bodily functions and processes. Micro means 'small' and we only need these in smaller amounts, but that doesn't mean they're not vitally important. (Remember learning about vitamin C and scurvy at school?)

PROTEINS: THE BUILDING BLOCKS

Proteins are made up of many building blocks called amino acids, which can then be classified as essential (they must be provided through diet) or non essential (they can be made by the human body). Protein plays an important role in the human body, being essential for growth and repair.

There are 20 amino acids in total, with nine of them being essential. The term 'complete protein' refers to a protein that contains all nine essential amino acids, such as the protein in meat, dairy products or soy.

However, incomplete sources of protein (such as a grain and a legume) can be combined to form a complete protein. Then they are known as 'complementary proteins'. And these don't need to be combined in the same meal; eating them over the course of a day is fine. This is especially important for people who aren't eating animal protein but are following a vegetarian or vegan diet.

CARBOHYDRATES: SIMPLE, OR NOT SO SIMPLE?

Carbohydrates can be divided into 'simple' sugars (glucose, fructose, galactose, maltose, sucrose and lactose) and 'complex' carbohydrates (starch and fibre). Glucose provides half the energy the brain uses daily and is, therefore, an essential carbohydrate.

When we eat carbohydrates, some of the glucose is used for immediate energy, while the remainder gets converted into glycogen and stored in our muscles. These are 'reserves' of energy that the body can use if food is scarce (something many of us rarely experience in the modern Western world). Good sources of carbohydrate include grains, fruit (fructose), vegetables, legumes and even milk (lactose).

The glycaemic index (GI) is a measure of the speed it takes individual carbohydrate foods to hit the bloodstream. The lower the GI of a food, the slower it releases glucose, the steadier and more sustained the energy release into the body. At the other end of the scale, foods with a high GI release glucose quickly and cause sudden spikes in blood sugar levels. Following a low GI diet is essential in the management of diabetes.

HEY, FATTY

Fats often get a bad rap, but in moderation they are essential for our health. Dietary fats and oils (triglycerides) fall into two broad categories: saturated and unsaturated fats. The fats found in food always contain a combination of both saturated and unsaturated fatty acids, but in differing ratios.

Unsaturated fats can be further classified as monounsaturated or polyunsaturated, and there are two types of polyunsaturated fats: omega-3 and omega-6 fatty acids. Mono and polyunsaturated fats are liquid at room temperature (olive oil and grapeseed oil, for example), while saturated fats are generally solid at room temperature (butter, lard, coconut oil and the fat on meat).

FOOD FOR ADDED LIFE

It has been proved over and over in nutritional and medical studies that the single most important thing we can do to improve our overall nutrition is to eat a diet rich in whole foods. And that shouldn't be difficult!

Think fresh fruit, veggies, nuts, seeds, eggs, whole grains and fresh meat. Whole foods are foods that are as close to their natural state as possible. They are unprocessed and unrefined, or have undergone only minimal processing, and don't include additives or artificial ingredients. This is where that popular mantra 'don't eat any food your grandparents wouldn't recognise' can come in handy as a checkpoint.

But why are they so good? It seems logical that if a food is still in its whole state, it contains the full array of nutrients (macro and micro) that nature gave it. For example, compare brown rice to white rice. Brown rice consists of the whole grain of rice – only the inedible outer husk has been removed and the grain retains its nutrient-rich bran and germ. The rice is essentially unaltered. White rice, in contrast, has been both milled and polished to remove the bran layer and the germ, along with all the nutrients they contain. Brown rice is a whole food; white rice is a processed food.

So: if it's not a whole food, it's a processed food.

Whole foods are not only better for us than processed foods, they also taste better. Advertising (particularly expensive advertising by processed food companies) tries to persuade us otherwise, but microwave dinners and stretchy white bread can't compete with the sweet juiciness of seasonal fruit or the nutty chewiness of whole grains. And the more whole foods we can eat, the better it is for us.

THE FOOD GOOD GUYS

Antioxidants We all hear this term a lot and know it's good, but what does it really mean? Antioxidants are chemicals that interact with and neutralise free radicals. Free radicals are chemicals in the human body that have the ability to harm cells and, in large quantities, increase the risk of certain diseases. They are highly unstable and reactive, the products of our metabolism as well as environmental effects such as smoking and urban pollution. Problems can occur when free radicals get out of control in the body, but antioxidants can stabilise them, hence their link to disease prevention. Antioxidants can be made by the body (endogenous) or be provided by diet (exogenous). A diet high in antioxidants is therefore linked to a reduced risk of certain diseases.

Phytochemicals (also called phytonutrients) These chemicals are found in plants and can provide protection against certain diseases. Phytochemicals include plant pigments, flavonoids and polyphenols. They all have the ability to act as antioxidants.

Dietary fibre (soluble) This forms a thick gel-like substance and slows down digestion – it's great for heart health because it can assist in lowering blood cholesterol by binding with bile acids and increasing their extraction. Soluble fibre also slows the absorption of sugars and can have a probiotic effect, producing good bacteria as it ferments in the colon. Foods such as porridge (rolled) oats are a great source of soluble fibre.

Dietary fibre (insoluble) This is not soluble in water and, therefore, passes through the digestive tract intact and adds bulk in the large intestine, helping food pass through more quickly. Insoluble fibre is great for digestive health, can help constipation by assisting with the efficient removal of waste and can reduce the risk of colon cancer.

AND FOODS THAT DON'T ADD LIFE

The flip side of whole foods is processed foods. When we imagine processed foods, we tend to think of commercially made cakes, biscuits, crisps, fast food and so on. But, really, any food that has undergone any alteration from its natural state is a processed food.

Not all processed foods are created equal, of course; there are degrees of processing. White rice is not an unhealthy food, but when we choose white rice over brown we are missing out on valuable nutrients.

Some methods of processing can be very useful – for example, pressing olives to make olive oil. And not all processing means the loss of nutrients – think of milling whole grains into flour. But a good general rule for the bulk of your diet is to choose foods that have undergone as little processing as possible. Choose wholegrain flour over white (which has undergone further processing beyond milling) and plain natural yoghurt over the flavoured, sweetened pots.

In their 'extreme' (highly processed) form, processed foods lose much of their nutritional value. Some whole foods undergo so many processes in their journey from nature to the supermarket shelf that they end up virtually unrecognisable – many lollies, cereals, cakes, biscuits and muesli bars hide their food origins well.

THE USUAL SUSPECTS

As well as containing fewer nutrients, highly processed foods often hit us with a double whammy, by including other ingredients that have undesirable health effects:

Saturated fats These are the fats that are generally solid at room temperature. Think animal fats, like the fat on a steak, as well as oils such as coconut or palm oil. Saturated fats are traditionally linked to health issues such as increased risk of heart disease, cancer and other diseases. For this reason the current recommendation is that saturated fats make up no more then 10 per cent of our total energy intake: higher levels can lead to a risk of heart disease. Some of the most common sources of saturated fats are commercially made biscuits, cakes, pastries, pizzas, hamburgers and processed meats such as salami.

Trans fats Very low levels of trans fats occur naturally in dairy products and meat. But they can also be created artificially through a process called 'partial hydrogenation', which is widely used in the food industry to convert liquid vegetable oils into solid fats to thicken, harden and preserve food, extending its shelf life. Partially hydrogenated fats have become the main source of trans fats in most Western diets. They are used in many brands of crackers, chips, frozen foods with a crumb coating (such as fish or chicken), packet cake mixes, and doughnuts. Think of foods such as cakes and biscuits, which are traditionally made with butter and kept for just a few days before turning rancid: these can now be commercially made with trans fats and kept on the shelf for months.

Trans fats behave like saturated fats, raising bad cholesterol levels and lowering your good cholesterol. So, best to try to avoid any food that declares 'partially hydrogenated vegetable oil' in its ingredients list.

Sugar Where previous generations stirred a spoonful of sugar into a cup of coffee, or creamed it into butter to bake a cake, we are now eating far higher quantities of 'invisible' sugar added to processed foods before it even reaches us. Ingredients such as corn syrup, invert sugar, dextrose and high fructose corn syrup – all common on food labels – are all forms of sugar. They're added to many processed foods, including savoury ones such as tinned vegetables and tomato ketchup. Australians eat about 43 kg (95 lb) of sugar each per year, much of it hidden in processed foods.

Sugar has virtually no nutritional value but is high in kilojoules. Excess sugar can contribute to obesity and other health issues such as diabetes and tooth decay.

Salt Sodium chloride, or salt, occurs naturally at low levels in almost all food and is also used extensively in the food processing world to enhance flavour (most of us just adore salt) and as a preservative. Where previous generations might have scattered a little salt onto their food at the table, around 75 per cent of our salt intake today comes hidden in processed foods. High salt intake is linked to increased blood pressure and hypertension, which can then lead to cardiovascular disease.

FADS, FAKES AND PHILOSOPHIES

Health sells, and the health industry is big business. During my career in food publishing, I've seen more food fads and diets than I can remember. They often promise quick weight loss and limit certain foods, or rely heavily on a diet of just a few specific foods. (Cabbage soup or grapefruit, anyone?)

We all get drawn to quick fixes and want to believe in miracle solutions. It's easy to be swept away by the promise of losing 5 kg (11 lb) in a week, or of solving all our health problems by cutting out a certain food group. If only it was that easy. The one thing all fad diets have in common is that they don't work over the long term. Good nutrition and the benefits of eating well require balanced eating over the course of a week, a month and a year. I am highly sceptical of any philosophy that eliminates entire food groups, demonises certain foods or consists of drinking all your meals.

IT'S ALL ON THE LABEL

Food packaging, like all other forms of marketing, is designed to be persuasive and appeal to our emotions. In Australia food labelling is regulated but still doesn't always tell the whole story. For example, a product can be labelled 'reduced fat' but it could still be relatively high in fat – it simply needs to be a certain percentage lower in fat than the full-fat version. Similarly, a product labelled 'low-fat' will indeed be low in fat – but it might make up for that by being packed with salt and sugar to replace some of its flavour.

I can't emphasise how important it is to read the label, but by 'label' I mean the ingredients list and the nutrition panel, not the claims such as 'low fat' and 'reduced sugar'. The ingredients list and the nutrition panel provide valuable straightforward information that help us make informed decisions.

The best way to compare the nutritive value and kilojoule count of processed foods is to look at the 'per 100 g' column. The 'per serve' column is less useful because the given serving size can be unrealistically small: who eats only half a small tub of yoghurt in one sitting? By comparing 100 g quantities for all foods you are levelling the playing field.

And, of course, reading the label is also critical when it comes to choosing foods that meet your own ethical standards, such as free-range, grass-fed or organic foods.

IF I COULD SAY JUST THREE THINGS...

- Eat more whole foods and less processed food. This is the single most important way to improve diet.
- Keep an inquiring mind and question the credibility of food fads. Good nutrition doesn't come from individual 'superfoods' or excluding food groups: it's a result of overall food intake. So, educate yourself about healthy eating. Knowledge is power.
- Whole foods are delicious foods. Eating a healthy diet based on whole foods doesn't mean depriving yourself, counting calories or restricting enjoyment. It means eating well and loving it.

GRAINS

GRAINS

Grains are an integral part of today's modern diet, just as they have been for thousands of years. They are the seeds of certain plants whose hard inedible husks or outer layers have been removed, leaving the edible grain kernels.

ARE GRAINS GOOD FOR US?

Grains are a great source of carbohydrate energy. They often make up the main 'energy source' of the meal: the bread, pasta or rice etc that fuels us. But grains don't need to be just the fillers on the plate: they can be vital and delicious sources of nutrients, too.

SO, HOW MANY SERVES SHOULD WE BE EATING?

Dietary guidelines around the world vary considerably, with the recommended serves per day ranging from three up to seven or more (for pregnant women or breastfeeding mothers). The mid point is somewhere around four–five serves per day. Obviously our daily needs will vary depending upon our age, activity level and so on. But the one thing all the guidelines have in common is that they show we should be increasing our consumption of whole grains over refined grains.

AND WHAT IS A SERVE OF GRAINS?

- 1 slice (40 g/1¹/₂ oz) bread
- ¹/₄ cup (30 g/1 oz) muesli
- ²/₃ cup (30 g/1 oz) cereal flakes
- ¹/₂ cup cooked porridge (oatmeal)
- ¹/₂ roll or flat bread
- ¹/₂ cup (about 100 g/3¹/₂ oz) cooked grain (such as rice, pasta, couscous or buckwheat)
- 3 slices (about 30 g/1 oz) crispbread

WHOLE GRAIN, HEALTHY GRAIN

Whole grains comprise all three parts of the grain: the endosperm (the starchy component), the bran (the fibre layer) and the germ (the protein, fat and mineral component). In contrast, refined grains have had the bran and germ removed, leaving only the starchy endosperm. Whole wheat consists of 83 per cent endosperm, but also 14.5 per cent bran and 2.5 per cent germ. The bran and germ, as well as being high in fibre, provide B vitamins and omega-3 and -6 fatty acids.

Many of the grains we eat are available in both whole and refined forms. Think brown rice (a whole grain) versus white rice (refined), or wholemeal (whole grain) wheat flour versus white wheat flour (refined). Refined grains that have had the bran and germ removed are mainly starch and good for a quick energy hit, but they lack the valuable nutrients from the bran and germ. These nutrients can't be returned during processing, so refined bread or pasta labelled 'added fibre' is still comparatively inferior. If you are going to eat grains, it makes sense to choose whole grains, to reap the full nutritional benefits they offer. Diets rich in whole grains are linked to health benefits including:

Heart health Whole grains rich in soluble fibre can be effective in reducing blood cholesterol. Whole grains are also linked to reduced blood pressure, reduced risk of stroke and healthier arteries.

Weight control The high fibre content of whole grains can increase satiety, making you feel full for longer and, therefore, eat less overall.

Blood sugar management Whole grains are rich in dietary fibre. Soluble fibre slows the release of sugars in the blood and is especially of benefit to those with diabetes. Many whole grains also have a low GI.

Disease prevention Whole grains contain phytochemicals and antioxidants that protect cells from damage and might reduce the risk of certain cancers. The insoluble fibre content of grains is linked to a reduced risk of colon cancer.

REFINED GRAINS: 'A WOLF IN SHEEP'S CLOTHING'

Refined grains tend to be used in processed foods, such as biscuits, cakes, snack bars or refined bread. They also appear in more surprising places, such as commercially made sauces, confectionery, yoghurts with additives, and even foods like burger patties or sausages.

Like all processed foods, these tend to be high in added fats, sugars or sodium (or all three), so they are not nutritious choices. Once again, we really need to read labels, to make ourselves aware of what the food actually contains. For example, the difference between commercially made muesli bars is astounding. A few brands provide bars with only five or six ingredients, all items you would probably find in your pantry. Other brands contain up to 15 ingredients you have never heard of and wouldn't want in your child's lunch box. Just because some thing is labelled 'healthy' or 'added whole grains' does not mean it doesn't also contain a lot of unnecessary additives. Read the label.

THE 'G WORD'

Gluten is a protein found in wheat, barley, rye and oats and some people react badly to eating it. In its most extreme form, gluten intolerance is known as coeliac disease, an autoimmune reaction that causes damage to the small bowel and can bring on a host of symptoms. In its lesser form, gluten sensitivity, people may suffer from various gastrointestinal issues, which are relieved by removing gluten from their diet. It is important to note that even if you're following a gluten-free diet, you should choose gluten-free *whole* grains. Gluten-free products can also be packed with highly processed grains and starches, and therefore have a high GI and lack nutrition.

WHOLE GRAINS WITH GLUTEN

Barley With a slightly chewy texture and delicious nutty taste, barley has an extremely low GI, so it's ideal for those on a low GI diet or with diabetes. It's packed with beta-glucan soluble fibre, which is linked to a reduced risk of heart disease. Barley is also a very good source of selenium and a good source of phosphorous, copper and manganese.

Farro An ancient variety of wheat, farro is also known as emmer wheat. Like spelt, it's easier to digest than common wheat, because its gluten molecules are not as strong, but it isn't suitable for those with coeliac disease. Farro is rich in fibre, protein, magnesium, niacin and zinc, as well as disease-fighting phytonutrients and antioxidants.

Freekeh Freekeh is wheat picked while it's still green and is therefore higher in nutrients. It contains higher levels of protein, dietary fibre, calcium, potassium, iron and zinc than ripe wheat. Wholegrain freekeh has a low GI and is available whole or cracked; the cracked form cooks more quickly.

Kamut (khorsan) Another ancient heirloom variety of wheat, this has a rich nutty taste. It is higher in protein than common wheat, as well as in several vitamins and minerals including selenium, magnesium and zinc. It may be easier to digest than common wheat for anyone with mild wheat intolerance.

Oats With more soluble fibre (beta-glucans) than any other grain, oats have been proven to help lower cholesterol. They can assist in reducing blood sugar and they contain iron, manganese, zinc, vitamin E, folate, B vitamins and antioxidants beneficial for health.

Spelt An ancient wholegrain variety of wheat, spelt has a delicious nutty taste. It's gentler on the digestion than regular wheat, so some people with mild wheat intolerance can actually tolerate spelt. Spelt is rich in vitamin B_2, vitamin B_3, dietary fibre, manganese, phosphorus, niacin, thiamin and copper, and it contains more protein and fats than common wheat. Spelt flour can be substituted for regular wheat flour in most baking recipes.

Wheat Whole wheat consists of the germ, bran and endosperm of the wheat grain (or wheat berry); only the inedible outer husk has been removed. Wholegrain wheat has a nutty flavour and texture and is rich in fibre, B vitamins and magnesium.

WHOLE GRAINS WITHOUT GLUTEN

Amaranth Grown by the Aztecs, this tiny, highly nutritious pseudo-grain has a low GI and is packed with calcium, iron, magnesium, manganese, phosphorus, B vitamins and vitamin E. It's a pseudo-grain because it's technically a seed but is closer in nutrition to a grain. Amaranth is a little trickier to cook with than, say, quinoa, and it has an earthy taste that some people find quite strong.

Brown rice Brown rice retains the nutrient-rich bran and germ, so it is considerably more nutritious than white rice. An excellent source of carbohydrate, brown rice is rich in dietary fibre and takes longer to digest than white rice. It's an excellent source of the trace mineral manganese and the minerals magnesium and selenium.

Buckwheat This ancient pseudo-grain from South-East Asia has a unique triangular shape, is a source of complete plant protein and is gluten free. It is rich in the nutrients manganese and magnesium, and a good source of niacin, folate, iron, zinc, copper, selenium and phosphorous. Buckwheat is the main ingredient in soba noodles. Some brands of soba also contain wheat flour, so check the label if you're going gluten free.

Millet A small grain thought to have originated in Africa, millet is gluten free and known for being gentle on the digestion. Also highly nutritious, millet is a good

source of manganese and contains a moderate amount of dietary fibre. It also contains phosphorus, zinc, copper and various disease-fighting phytochemicals.

Quinoa This ancient pseudo-grain from the Andes is a rich source of complete plant protein. It is also gluten free, high in dietary fibre and a good source of nutrients such as manganese, phosphorous, magnesium and folate. Quinoa is extremely nutritious, versatile to use and quick to prepare, which explains its current popularity.

Sorghum Native to Africa, this has a mild, slightly sweet taste, is highly nutritious and is a good source of iron, niacin and phosphorus. Sorghum flour is a favourite of mine for gluten-free baking.

AND WHAT ABOUT THE ANTI-GRAINS LOBBY?

Grains, particularly wheat, seem to be under the spotlight as grain-free diets such as the paleo diet have become popular. But is this criticism of an entire food group deserved?

It all comes back to balance and, most importantly, to choosing whole grains over processed. No one food group should dominate our diet, but it is very easy to fall into a habit of eating too many processed grains – especially wheat – without realising.

This food routine might look familiar:

- Breakfast: packet cereal with milk, and toast
- Morning snack: processed muesli bar or muffin
- Lunch: sandwich made with white bread
- Afternoon snack: biscuits with a cup of tea
- Dinner: pasta with meat sauce

Obviously, what's listed above is not a balanced diet. The key to eating grains, like any food group, is not to consume just one or two members of the group (say, wheat and rice) but to eat a variety of grains, just as we do with fruit and vegetables.

We also need to ensure that we are eating quality grains; that is, whole grains. Whole grains cannot be compared with their highly processed counterparts. And, possibly most importantly, we need to eat them in moderation and as part of a balanced meal. So often, our serving size is simply too large.

To try to counteract our supersized portions, I like to imagine a dinner plate. At least half the plate should be vegetables/salad, and one quarter of the plate should be lean protein (fish, tofu, meat, egg), leaving the final quarter for a serve of whole grains or a carbohydrate-rich vegetable (such as sweet potato).

Therefore, if you're going to have pasta for dinner, make the pasta wholegrain, serve it with a sauce loaded with vegetables and some protein, skip the garlic bread and make the serving size appropriate (about 60 g/2¼ oz dried weight per person). Or, if you're having a sandwich for lunch, make the bread wholegrain packed with seeds, add some lean protein and then fill the sandwich up with salad veggies such as carrot, cucumber, spinach and beetroot.

After all, not only have we been eating grains for thousands of years, but many of the world's most highly regarded diets in terms of health benefits, such as the Mediterranean diet, are rich in whole grains.

HOW CAN WE EAT A WIDER, HEALTHIER VARIETY OF GRAINS?

Breakfast cereal Swap commercially made cereal, which is often loaded with sugar, for porridge made from wholegrain oats, quinoa, millet or amaranth. Or make your own granola or muesli.

Bread Look for bread with the labels 'wholegrain' and 'wholemeal'. Wholegrain bread is made from wholemeal flour with grains added to make it more nutritious. Bread labelled 'multigrain' is often made from white flour.

Soups Add a handful of farro, barley, freekeh or millet to your favourite soup to give it extra body and texture.

Flour Replace some of your regular wheat flour with wholegrain spelt, buckwheat, millet, quinoa or sorghum flour.

Salads Freekeh, farro, brown rice, millet, buckwheat, quinoa and barley all make delicious salad grains, with their nutty flavour and al dente texture.

Stir-fries and curries Brown rice, quinoa or barley is perfect with your favourite stir-fry, or instead of white rice in fried rice. Steamed quinoa is delicious with curries – it soaks up all the great flavours.

Pilafs Try making a pilaf or risotto using barley, quinoa or millet.

Pasta Swap wheat pasta for wholegrain, spelt or kamut pasta, or try buckwheat for a gluten-free option.

Stuffings Swap the breadcrumbs or rice in your favourite stuffing for quinoa, millet, barley or freekeh.

TO SUM IT ALL UP

- Grains are a nutritious part of a balanced diet but refined cannot be considered the same as whole grains. We should all aim to eat fewer refined grains and more whole grains.
- If you refine the grain by stripping away its fibre and germ, then you're pretty much eating it just for its energy – think highly processed starch versus nutritious food.
- Refined grains are often used in highly processed snack foods that are also high in fat, sugar and salt.
- Consumption of whole grains can be linked to better heart health, healthy blood sugar levels, weight management and disease prevention.
- There are many different grains, all with unique properties. We should aim to eat a wide variety, rather than relying on wheat, rice and corn.

OAT AND RICOTTA PANCAKES
WITH AVOCADO SALSA

These light, wheat-free pancakes are based on protein-rich ricotta and finely processed oats, which are an excellent source of soluble fibre. For a sweet version, serve the pancakes with chopped walnuts and a drizzle of honey.

Preparation time: 15 minutes
Cooking time: 10 minutes
Serves 4

100 g (3^1/$_2$ oz/1 cup) rolled (porridge) oats

230 g (8 oz/1 cup) ricotta cheese

4 eggs

60 ml (2 fl oz/^{1}/$_4$ cup) milk

1 teaspoon baking powder

150 g (5^1/$_2$ oz) sweet potato, finely grated

Olive oil, for brushing

50 g (1^3/$_4$ oz/1 cup) baby English spinach leaves

AVOCADO SALSA

200 g (7 oz) cherry tomatoes, halved

1 small avocado, diced

2 tablespoons chopped herbs, such as chives, basil or flat-leaf (Italian) parsley

2 teaspoons olive oil

For the avocado salsa, toss together the tomatoes, avocado, herbs and olive oil.

Process the oats in a food processor until they form a coarse flour. Add the ricotta, eggs, milk and baking powder and process until smooth. Stir in the sweet potato.

Heat a large non-stick frying pan over medium–high heat and brush with oil. Ladle ^{1}/$_3$ cup of batter per pancake into the pan. Cook for 2 minutes each side or until golden and cooked through. Keep warm while you cook the rest, adding a little more oil if necessary.

Serve 2 pancakes per person, topped with avocado salsa and baby spinach leaves.

BUCKWHEAT, CHICKEN AND GRAPE SALAD
WITH HAZELNUTS

*Buckwheat, a pseudo-grain like quinoa and amaranth, is gluten free and has
a delicious earthy taste that teams well with sweet grapes and nutty hazelnuts.
Toasting the buckwheat really brings out its flavour.*

Preparation time: 15 minutes
Cooking time: 25 minutes
Serves 4

50 g (1³/₄ oz/¹/₃ cup) hazelnuts

150 g (5¹/₂ oz/³/₄ cup) raw buckwheat

2 x 200 g (7 oz) chicken breast fillets

1 tablespoon olive oil, plus extra
for brushing

2 bunches asparagus (about 16 spears)

200 g (7 oz) red seedless grapes,
halved

¹/₃ cup chopped herbs, such as parsley,
chives and mint, plus extra to garnish

1 tablespoon white balsamic vinegar

1 tablespoon lemon juice

1 teaspoon honey

Preheat the oven to 180°C (350°F). Lightly toast the hazelnuts on a
baking tray for 8–10 minutes, then wrap the hot nuts in a tea towel
and rub off the papery skins. Chop the nuts coarsely.

Heat a large saucepan over medium–high heat. Add the buckwheat
and cook, stirring, for 3–4 minutes or until fragrant. Add 500 ml
(17 fl oz/2 cups) water and bring to the boil. Cover, reduce the heat
to low and simmer for 12 minutes or until just tender (be careful not
to overcook). Rinse under cold running water and drain well.

Slice each chicken breast horizontally through the middle so you have
4 thin fillets. Heat a chargrill pan over medium–high heat. Brush the
chicken with extra oil and cook for 2–3 minutes each side or until lightly
charred and cooked through. Brush the asparagus with oil and cook for
1–2 minutes each side or until just tender. Cool, then thinly slice the
chicken and cut the asparagus into short lengths.

Combine the buckwheat, chicken, asparagus, grapes, herbs and half
the hazelnuts in a large bowl. Whisk together the vinegar, olive oil,
lemon juice and honey to make a dressing, and gently toss through the
salad. Serve garnished with the remaining hazelnuts and extra herbs.

STIR-FRIED MILLET
WITH CORN, GAI LARN AND CAPSICUM

Millet grain has a buttery, almost corn-like flavour that works deliciously in this version of 'fried rice'. It also has close to twice the fibre and protein of white rice and it's gluten free.

Preparation time: 20 minutes
Cooking time: 35 minutes
Serves 4

160 g (5³⁄₄ oz/³⁄₄ cup) millet

2 eggs, lightly beaten

2 teaspoons peanut or macadamia oil

1¹⁄₂ tablespoons low-salt tamari (see tip)

2 teaspoons lime juice

1 teaspoon brown sugar

1 red onion, finely chopped

2 garlic cloves, crushed

2 teaspoons finely grated ginger

1 long red chilli, seeded and finely chopped

175 g (6 oz) red, green and yellow small capsicums (peppers), seeded and quartered

2 cobs corn, kernels removed

1 bunch gai larn (Chinese broccoli), stalks and leaves cut into 4 cm (1¹⁄₂ inch) lengths

2 tablespoons unsalted roasted cashews, chopped

Heat a large saucepan over medium–high heat, add the millet and cook, stirring, for 3 minutes or until fragrant. Add 500 ml (17 fl oz/2 cups) water and bring to the boil. Reduce the heat to low, cover and simmer for 15–20 minutes or until the water has been absorbed. Remove from the heat and leave to steam for 5 minutes.

Season the eggs with sea salt and freshly ground black pepper. Heat 1 teaspoon of the oil in a large non-stick wok or frying pan over medium heat. Add half the egg, swirl to cover the base and cook for 2 minutes or until set. Carefully loosen the edge and turn out onto a board. Leave to cool while you cook the rest of the egg. Roll up the 2 omelettes and cut them into thin strips.

Stir together the tamari, lime juice and sugar in a small bowl until the sugar has dissolved.

Heat the remaining oil in a wok over high heat. Add the onion and stir-fry for 2 minutes. Add the garlic, ginger and chilli and stir-fry for 30 seconds or until aromatic. Add the capsicum, corn and gai larn stalks and stir-fry for 2 minutes or until almost tender. Add the gai larn leaves and stir-fry for 1 minute.

Add the millet and tamari mixture and stir-fry until heated through. Serve topped with omelette strips and cashews.

✛ TIP ✛
This recipe is gluten free if you use gluten-free tamari.

QUINOA PILAF
WITH THREE PEAS, ALMONDS AND LEMON

A pilaf is so much easier to make than a risotto because you don't have to stand over it stirring! Quinoa's high protein content and complete amino acid profile make it a fantastic food for vegetarians, and almonds increase the protein content here, too.

Preparation time: 20 minutes
Cooking time: 25 minutes
Serves 4

2 teaspoons olive oil

1 onion, finely chopped

2 garlic cloves, crushed

2 teaspoons thinly sliced lemon zest, plus extra to garnish

250 ml (9 fl oz/1 cup) home-made or low-salt vegetable stock

200 g (7 oz/1 cup) quinoa, rinsed and drained

140 g (5 oz/1 cup) podded fresh or frozen peas

150 g (5 1/2 oz/2 cups) sugar snap peas, sliced

150 g (5 1/2 oz) snow peas (mangetout), sliced

1 tablespoon snipped chives

2 tablespoons chopped flat-leaf (Italian) parsley

35 g (1 1/4 oz/1/4 cup) slivered almonds, toasted

Marinated feta cheese, to serve (optional)

Heat half the oil in a large saucepan over medium heat. Add the onion and cook, stirring occasionally, for 5 minutes or until softened. Add the garlic and lemon zest and stir for 1 minute.

Add the stock, quinoa and 160 ml (5 1/4 fl oz/2/3 cup) water and bring to the boil. Reduce the heat to low, cover and simmer for 12 minutes or until the water has almost evaporated (see tip). Stir in the peas, cover and cook for 2 minutes or until the water has evaporated.

Remove from the heat, add the sugar snaps and snow peas, cover and leave to steam for 3 minutes.

Stir in the chives and half the parsley. Season with black pepper and garnish with almonds, remaining parsley and extra lemon zest. Top with a little feta.

✦ TIP ✦

The trick with this pilaf is to keep the grains slightly al dente, so the recipe calls for slightly less liquid than you'd usually use to cook the quinoa.

FREEKEH, BROCCOLI AND CHICKPEA SALAD
(see recipe page 24)

SPICED LENTILS AND RICE
WITH SPINACH AND
CARAMELISED ONIONS
(see recipe page 25)

FREEKEH, BROCCOLI AND CHICKPEA SALAD

Freekeh is wheat that has been picked while it's still green and then roasted. Nutritionally, it leaves regular wheat in the shade: it contains more protein and dietary fibre, as well as calcium, potassium, iron and zinc.

Preparation time: 15 minutes
Cooking time: 15 minutes
Serves 4

300 g (10$\frac{1}{2}$ oz) broccoli, trimmed, cut into small florets

Olive oil spray

250 g (9 oz) cherry tomatoes, halved

120 g (4$\frac{1}{4}$ oz/$\frac{3}{4}$ cup) cracked freekeh (see tip)

400 g (14 oz) can chickpeas, rinsed and drained

$\frac{1}{3}$ cup basil leaves, coarsely chopped, plus extra leaves to garnish

$\frac{1}{4}$ cup flat-leaf (Italian) parsley leaves, coarsely chopped

2 tablespoons sunflower seeds, lightly toasted

1 tablespoon balsamic vinegar

1 tablespoon olive oil

2 teaspoons lemon juice

Preheat the oven to 200°C (400°F) and line a large baking tray with baking paper. Spread the broccoli on the tray, spray lightly with olive oil and cook for 5 minutes. Add the tomatoes and cook for 8–10 minutes or until the tomatoes are wilted and the broccoli is tender.

Meanwhile, cook the freekeh in a large saucepan of lightly salted boiling water for 12–15 minutes or until al dente. Rinse under cold water, drain well and squeeze out as much water as possible. Transfer to a large bowl with the roasted vegetables, chickpeas, herbs and sunflower seeds.

Whisk together the vinegar, olive oil and lemon juice, pour the dressing over the salad and toss to combine. Scatter with extra basil.

✦ **TIP** ✦

Cracked freekeh are grains that have been split during processing. The cracked variety cooks in just over half the time of whole freekeh.

(pictured page 22)

SPICED LENTILS AND RICE
WITH SPINACH AND CARAMELISED ONIONS

This version of the traditional Lebanese dish called mujadara *contains the winning combo of wholegrain brown rice and lentils, which together make a complete protein. It's delicious as a vegetarian main course or served with grilled lamb.*

Preparation time: 15 minutes
Cooking time: 30 minutes
Serves 4

170 g (6 oz/3/4 cup) brown lentils, rinsed

150 g (51/2 oz/3/4 cup) brown rice

2 tablespoons olive oil

3 red onions, thinly sliced

2 garlic cloves, crushed

1 teaspoon ground cumin

1 teaspoon ground coriander

150 g (51/2 oz) English spinach, coarsely chopped

Lemon juice, to taste

Natural yoghurt, to serve

Cook the lentils and rice in a large saucepan of boiling water for 25 minutes or until just tender. Drain well.

Meanwhile, heat 1 tablespoon of the oil in a large non-stick frying pan over low heat. Add the onions and cook, stirring occasionally, for 15–20 minutes or until golden and caramelised.

Heat the remaining oil in a large saucepan over medium heat. Add the garlic and spices and cook, stirring, for 1 minute or until fragrant. Add half the caramelised onion and cook for 1 minute. Add the rice and lentils and stir to heat through. Stir in the spinach and add lemon juice to taste.

Serve the lentils and rice topped with the remaining caramelised onions and a dollop of yoghurt.

(pictured page 23)

SOOTHING CHICKEN SOUP
WITH BARLEY AND GREENS

Nothing beats home-made chicken soup on a cold night, or when you're not feeling one hundred per cent. The secret to a good soup lies in making your own stock, which will be full of flavour and without the high levels of sodium found in commercial products. Chicken Marylands are ideal for stock because they give you all the flavour of the bones as well as meat to shred and add to the soup.

Preparation time: 20 minutes
Cooking time: 1 hour 50 minutes
Serves 4

1 tablespoon olive oil

2 large chicken Marylands (about 800 g/1 lb 12 oz), skin removed

1 onion, coarsely chopped

8 black peppercorns

4 celery stalks, diced

1 leek, cut into thin rounds

1 small fennel bulb, finely chopped

3 garlic cloves, thinly sliced

1 bay leaf

100 g (3¹/2 oz/¹/2 cup) pearl barley, rinsed

1 zucchini (courgette), diced

75 g (2³/4 oz/about ¹/2 bunch) trimmed silverbeet (Swiss chard), chopped

¹/2 cup flat-leaf (Italian) parsley leaves

1 tablespoon thinly sliced lemon zest

Heat 2 teaspoons of the oil in a large saucepan over high heat and cook the chicken for 2–3 minutes on each side until golden. Add the onion, peppercorns and 2 litres (70 fl oz/8 cups) water. Bring to the boil, partially cover and simmer for 1 hour. Strain the stock, discarding the onion and peppercorns, and set the chicken aside to cool.

Clean the saucepan and return it to medium heat. Add the remaining oil, celery, leek and fennel and cook, stirring, for 5 minutes or until softened. Add the garlic and bay leaf and stir for 1 minute.

Add the barley and 1.5 litres (52 fl oz/6 cups) of the stock. Bring to the boil, reduce the heat to low–medium and simmer for 30 minutes or until the barley is tender.

Meanwhile, dice the chicken meat. Add the chicken, zucchini and silverbeet to the soup. Simmer for 10 minutes or until the vegetables are tender. Season to taste.

Mix together the parsley and lemon zest and scatter over the soup just before serving.

+ TIP +

This soup can be frozen in airtight containers for up to 3 months.

WARM BARLEY AND ROASTED MUSHROOM SALAD
WITH GOAT'S CURD

Pearl barley has a glycaemic index (GI) of just 25. Its high soluble fibre content slows the body's absorption of sugar, which lowers the overall GI value of a meal. Mushrooms, often referred to as 'meat for vegetarians', are one of the best plant sources of niacin, and they even contain a small amount of vitamin B_{12}, which is otherwise found almost exclusively in animal sources.

Preparation time: 15 minutes
Cooking time: 30 minutes
Serves 4

150 g (5^1/$_2$ oz/^{3}/$_4$ cup) pearl barley

500 g (1 lb 2 oz) mixed mushrooms, coarsely chopped

Olive oil spray

2 tablespoons currants

1 tablespoon balsamic vinegar

2 teaspoons olive oil

1 leek, thinly sliced

2 garlic cloves, crushed

2 teaspoons chopped thyme

2 tablespoons chopped flat-leaf (Italian) parsley

120 g (4^1/$_4$ oz/^{1}/$_2$ cup) goat's curd or fresh ricotta cheese

2 tablespoons walnuts, toasted and coarsely chopped

Cook the barley in a large saucepan of boiling water for 25 minutes or until al dente. Rinse under cold running water and drain well.

Meanwhile, preheat the oven to 200°C (400°F) and line a large baking tray with baking paper. Spread the mushrooms on the tray and spray with olive oil. Roast for 20 minutes or until golden and tender.

Combine the currants and vinegar in a small bowl and set aside for 10 minutes to soften the currants.

Heat the oil in a large non-stick frying pan over medium heat. Add the leek and cook, stirring occasionally, for 5 minutes or until softened. Add the garlic and thyme and cook for 1 minute or until fragrant. Add the cooked barley, roasted mushrooms, currants and vinegar and cook, stirring, for 2 minutes or until heated through. Stir in the parsley and season to taste with sea salt and freshly ground black pepper.

To serve, spread a little goat's curd on each plate. Top with the warm barley salad and sprinkle with the toasted walnuts.

ROASTED GARLIC, PARMESAN
AND OLIVE FLAT BREAD

(see recipe page 32)

BEEF AND FARRO
TAGINE WITH PRESERVED
LEMON SALAD

(see recipe page 33)

ROASTED GARLIC, PARMESAN AND OLIVE FLAT BREAD

Flour made from the whole sorghum grain has a neutral, slightly sweet flavour that lends itself perfectly to baking. Highly nutritious, it has a lower GI than many flours, is a good source of fibre and is naturally gluten free.

Preparation time: 15 minutes,
    plus 30 minutes proving
Cooking time: 1 hour 10 minutes
Serves 10–12

2 garlic bulbs

2 tablespoons olive oil, plus extra for drizzling

3 teaspoons honey

7 g (2 teaspoons) dried yeast

225 g (8 oz/1¹/2 cups) sorghum flour

70 g (2¹/2 oz/¹/2 cup) millet flour

¹/2 teaspoon xanthan gum

50 g (1³/4 oz/¹/2 cup) almond meal

35 g (1¹/4 oz/¹/3 cup) finely grated parmesan cheese (see tips)

2 eggs, lightly beaten

10 large green olives, pitted

Rosemary sprigs, to garnish

Preheat the oven to 180°C (350°F). Slice the top from each garlic bulb, leaving the cloves attached at the base, and remove the excess papery skin, leaving at least one layer. Place each bulb on a piece of foil, drizzle with a little oil and wrap to enclose in foil. Bake for 45 minutes or until the garlic is very tender and light golden. Cool completely and then squeeze the garlic pulp from the skins.

Whisk the honey and yeast with 125 ml (4 fl oz/¹/2 cup) water and leave in a warm place for 10 minutes or until frothy. Meanwhile, line a baking tray with baking paper.

Sift the flours and xanthan gum into a bowl. Stir in the almond meal, parmesan, roasted garlic pulp and a pinch of sea salt. Make a well in the centre, add the egg, oil and yeast mixture and stir with a wooden spoon to form a soft dough. Turn out onto a work surface and knead for 30 seconds or until smooth. Press the dough into a 30 cm (12 inch) round on the tray. Cover with a damp tea towel and leave in a warm place for 30 minutes or until slightly risen.

Press dimples into the dough with your fingers, then press the olives into the dough. Decorate with rosemary and drizzle with a little extra oil. Bake for 20–25 minutes or until golden brown and crisp. Cool for 5 minutes, then transfer to a wire rack. Serve warm.

+ TIPS +

For a vegetarian version, use parmesan made with non-animal rennet.

The bread is best served as soon as it's made, but it can be reheated.

(pictured page 30)

BEEF AND FARRO TAGINE
WITH PRESERVED LEMON SALAD

Farro, an ancient variety of wheat, has a delicious nutty taste and a slightly chewy texture. Like spelt, farro is more easily digested than regular wheat, which makes it suitable for some people on wheat-restricted diets.

Preparation time: 20 minutes
Cooking time: 2 hours
Serves 4

100 g (3^1/$_2$ oz/^{1}/$_2$ cup) raw farro

1 tablespoon olive oil

500 g (1 lb 2 oz) lean blade steak, cut into 2 cm (^{3}/$_4$ inch) cubes

1 large onion, diced

2 celery stalks, diced

2 garlic cloves, thinly sliced

2 teaspoons ground cumin

2 teaspoons ground coriander

2 teaspoons sweet paprika

1 teaspoon ground cinnamon

500 ml (17 fl oz/2 cups) home-made or low-salt beef stock

300 g (10^1/$_2$ oz) peeled pumpkin (winter squash), cut into 2 cm (^{3}/$_4$ inch) cubes

50 g (1^3/$_4$ oz) dried pitted dates, chopped

PRESERVED LEMON SALAD

^{1}/$_2$ cup flat-leaf (Italian) parsley leaves

^{1}/$_3$ cup coriander (cilantro) leaves

2 preserved lemon quarters, flesh and pith removed, zest thinly sliced

2 tablespoons slivered almonds, toasted

Heat a large non-stick frying pan over medium–high heat. Add the farro and cook, stirring, for 2–3 minutes or until fragrant and light golden (see tips).

Preheat the oven to 160°C (315°F). Heat half the oil in a large flameproof casserole dish over high heat. Brown the beef in two batches, stirring occasionally, for 2–3 minutes. Remove all the beef.

Reduce the heat to medium, add the remaining oil to the casserole dish and cook the onion and celery, stirring, for 6–7 minutes until softened. Add the garlic and spices and cook, stirring, for 1 minute or until fragrant. Return the beef to the casserole dish and stir in the farro, stock and 250 ml (9 fl oz/1 cup) water. Bring to the boil, then cover and put in the oven.

Cook for 1^1/$_4$ hours, then add the pumpkin and dates. Cover and cook for 30 minutes or until the beef is very tender. Season with sea salt and freshly ground black pepper.

Mix together all the ingredients for the preserved lemon salad and serve with the tagine.

✦ TIPS ✦

Farro is available raw or toasted. If you buy toasted farro, skip the first step.

This tagine is suitable to freeze without the preserved lemon salad. Freeze in an airtight container for up to 3 months.

(pictured page 31)

AMARANTH, ORANGE AND DARK CHOCOLATE BITES

I love something small and sweet after dinner and these choc bites are perfect. They're filled with crunchy puffed amaranth, coconut, almonds and bitter orange, and they're just the right size. To maximise the antioxidant benefits, use a dark chocolate that contains at least 70 per cent cocoa solids.

Preparation time: 15 minutes,
   plus 4 hours setting
Cooking time: 5 minutes
Makes about 20

55 g (2 oz/³/4 cup) shredded coconut

25 g (1 oz/¹/4 cup) flaked natural almonds

20 g (³/4 oz/³/4 cup) puffed amaranth

200 g (7 oz) dark chocolate (minimum 70 per cent cocoa solids), coarsely chopped

Thinly peeled zest of 1 orange, white pith removed, finely chopped

Lightly toast the coconut, almonds and puffed amaranth in a large frying pan over medium heat for 2–3 minutes. Set aside to cool.

Melt the chocolate by stirring in a heatproof bowl over a saucepan of gently simmering water (don't let the base of the bowl touch the water). Remove from the heat. Stir in the amaranth mixture and half the orange zest.

Line a large tray with baking paper. Spoon heaped teaspoons of the mixture onto the tray, then sprinkle the mounds with the remaining orange zest.

Set aside at room temperature for about 4 hours to set.

✦ TIP ✦

These choc bites will keep in an airtight container in a cool dark place for up to 1 month.

LEGUMES

LEGUMES

Legumes are delicious whole foods and of great nutritional importance throughout the world. All legumes are members of the Fabaceae family, with some 13,000 different species grown worldwide. All legumes produce seed-bearing pods and the seeds, when dried, are sometimes referred to as pulses. Legumes can also be eaten fresh, such as green beans, snow peas, sugar snap peas and borlotti beans.

ARE LEGUMES GOOD FOR US?

Legumes are nutritional powerhouses. Not only are they a valuable source of plant protein, they are also packed with dietary fibre, gluten free, low GI and a valuable source of several nutrients including:

- iron, needed to produce haemoglobin and transport oxygen around the body
- zinc, required for a healthy immune system, growth and metabolic processes
- magnesium, for healthy bones, muscle function and energy metabolism
- potassium, essential not only for fluid balance, but also to assist muscle function and metabolism
- B vitamins, for energy metabolism, growth and hormone function
- folate, for the healthy development of foetuses, required to make DNA, RNA and red blood cells

HOW MANY SERVES OF LEGUMES SHOULD WE EAT?

Legumes are so packed with nutrition that they are included in two of the main food groups. They are members of the vegetables group for their high levels of fibre, vitamins, minerals and antioxidants, and also grouped with lean meat, poultry, fish, eggs, tofu, nuts and seeds for their high protein content.

Dietary guidelines worldwide recommend at least five serves from the vegetables/legumes group every day. They also recommend eating one to three serves from the protein-rich food group. Most Australians aren't eating their five serves of vegetables/legumes.

AND WHAT IS A SERVE?

- 1 cup (about 150 g/5^1/2 oz) cooked legumes is considered one serve of protein.
- 1/2 cup (about 75 g/2^3/4 oz) cooked legumes is considered one serve of vegetables.

COMPLETE OR NOT COMPLETE?

Proteins are made up of many building blocks called amino acids. There are 20 amino acids, of which nine are 'essential' (our body can't make them, so we have to get them from food) and 11 are non-essential (the body can make these itself). A 'complete protein', such as meat or seafood, contains all the essential amino acids.

Legumes, apart from soy beans, do not contain all nine essential amino acids, so are incomplete proteins. Most grains (with the exception of a few of the pseudo-grains – quinoa and buckwheat) are also incomplete proteins. But when you combine a grain and a legume you end up with all nine essential amino acids, so together they provide a 'complete protein' source, particularly important for vegetarians and vegans. That's why traditional combos such as rice and beans, or lentils and bread, can be found in so many cultures. It's important to point out that these combinations don't need to be eaten in the same meal; over the course of your daily intake is fine.

LEGUMES FROM A TO Z

Adzuki beans Native to Asia, these small red beans have a distinctive white ridge on one side and are available dried or canned. Popular in Asian desserts, adzuki beans are also highly nutritious, being high in protein and fibre, low in fat, and rich in the minerals calcium, phosphorus and magnesium. They work beautifully with Japanese flavours.

Black beans Used extensively in South American cooking, these small shiny beans have a meaty flavour and creamy texture that makes them particularly satisfying in vegetarian dishes. Their colour comes from anthocyanin pigments, powerful antioxidants that may help prevent cancer and heart disease.

Borlotti beans These white beans with their distinctive red markings can be eaten immature (fresh) or mature (dried). Not just an excellent source of plant protein, they are also rich in dietary fibre and vitamin C and are a good source of folate, which is essential during pregnancy. Add them to Italian soup, risotto, pasta or salads.

Broad beans Also known as fava beans, broad beans can be eaten immature (fresh) or mature (dried). Immature broad beans can also be bought frozen, which is convenient because they have such a short season. Rich in protein (about 25 per cent), dietary fibre and slow-release carbohydrates, they are also high in vitamin A, which is essential for good eye health, and the B vitamins, important for energy production.

Chickpeas Originating in the Middle East, these nutty, buttery legumes have a low GI and are rich in protein and dietary fibre. They're also a valuable source of folate, manganese, copper, iron and phosphorus and their outer layer is loaded with antioxidants. Fabulous in curries, stews, salads and, of course, hummus.

Green beans Another member of the legume family eaten fresh, green beans are not only versatile, they are also high in protein and a rich source of vitamins K, C, folate and B_2, and vitamin A in the form of carotenoids. They have a low GI and kilojoule (calorie) count. Eat raw, lightly steamed or stir-fried.

Lentils (brown, red, green) Lentils come in different colours and sizes and pack a nutritional punch, with their protein content being among the highest of the legumes. Unlike other dried legumes, do not need presoaking, yet still cook relatively quickly. Lentils are packed with dietary fibre, both soluble and insoluble. Soluble fibre not only assists in reducing cholesterol levels, but can also help stabilise and regulate blood sugar levels. Lentils work beautifully with spices; use them in soups, salads, curries or dal.

Peas, dried and split These both come from a special variety of field peas that are either dried or have had their outer layer removed and been split. Dried peas are packed with soluble fibre (linked to reduced cholesterol levels) and insoluble fibre. Insoluble fibre can assist digestive disorders, such as irritable bowel syndrome and constipation, while solube fibre helps to stabilise blood sugar levels.

Peas, fresh Sugar snaps, snow peas (mangetout) and fresh green peas are all members of the legume family. Not as high in protein as dried legumes, they are still an excellent source of fibre, vitamin C and beta-carotene and a good source of potassium, niacin and folate. Ideal for salads, stir-fries and raw snacks.

Pinto beans Very popular in the US, these small oval beans with reddish brown splotches are the key ingredient in Mexican refried beans and burritos. Pinto beans are one of the most nutritious legumes. Packed with dietary fibre, they have a low GI, which helps to stabilise blood sugar levels and benefits heart health. They are rich in folate, magnesium and potassium.

Red kidney beans These dark red beans have a distinctive kidney shape, nutty flavour and creamy texture. They are a very good source of folate and manganese, essential for energy production. They are a great vegetarian source of iron, have a low GI and contain good quantities of magnesium and potassium. Use them in salads, curries, salads, tacos or dips.

Soy beans Almost legendary as a nutritious food for vegetarians, soy beans are a plant source of complete protein (meaning they contain all nine essential amino acids, just like meat and seafood). Soy beans are also a good source of B vitamins, potassium and zinc, and are low in saturated fat. They contain isoflavones, linked to health benefits such as easing menopausal symptoms in women and reducing the risk of osteoporosis and certain cancers. Soy beans can be bought in their dried mature form, or as fresh immature beans (edamame).

White beans (cannellini, butter, haricot) These three beans are all white skinned, have a creamy texture and are interchangeable in most recipes. All are rich in protein and fibre, folate and magnesium, and low in fat. Use them in salads, soups or traditional baked beans.

And some lesser known legumes The legume family is full of surprises – peanuts, lupins, alfalfa, indigenous Australian wattle seed, mesquite and even carob are all legumes. The one thing they have in common is that they are highly nutritious foods.

DRIED OR CANNED?

Dried legumes are my personal preference, because they tend to have a better texture after cooking than the canned version, and they're more economical too. I like to cook a large batch of beans, use half, then freeze the rest in meal-size portions in snaplock bags with a little of the cooking liquid. This way, they're ready to add to a curry or casserole with no pre-cooking required.

The canned version is convenient, though, and there's negligible nutritional difference between dried and canned, so it makes sense to have both on hand – in fact, canned legumes should be a staple in every pantry. They need just a rinse, and then you can throw them into soups, salads or stews. On the downside, they tend to contain added salt, and the amount varies a lot between brands. Check the labels and look for 'no added sodium'.

AND WHAT ABOUT FROZEN?

Some fresh legumes such as fresh peas, green beans, soy beans (edamame) and broad beans are also available frozen. As these legumes are quite dense and don't have a high water content, they freeze very successfully. Snap-frozen immediately after harvest, they are in fact often nutritionally superior to the fresh ones that have been hanging around in your crisper for more than a few days.

Legumes such as broad beans and peas have a very short season and can be expensive and hard to find, while the frozen packs are available all year round and at a consistent price. You will always find a bag of frozen peas and broad beans in my freezer, ready to throw into a curry, risotto or salad.

DIGESTIVE ISSUES?

Legumes have earned a bad reputation for causing digestive discomfort. If this happens to you, you'll know what I'm talking about! The culprits are carbohydrate sugars called oligosaccharides, which can cause symptoms such as abdominal bloating and wind. The good news is that most people can minimise or avoid these symptoms with a few simple tips:

- Soak. Always soak dried legumes (other than lentils) before cooking and try to change the soaking water a couple of times.
- Rinse. The key is to rinse dried legumes, both after soaking and after cooking. Also rinse canned legumes thoroughly before eating.
- Take your time. If legumes are problematic for you, add them to your diet gradually, so your body can slowly adjust. This should help to reduce symptoms.

HOW CAN WE INCLUDE MORE LEGUMES IN OUR DIET?

Considering legumes are so nutritious and we currently don't eat enough of them, what are some simple ways to include more in our daily diet?

Legumes for breakfast Make a batch of home-made baked beans and serve topped with a poached egg, or add a handful of red kidney beans or black beans to scrambled eggs or an omelette.

Salads and wraps Canned legumes make a super-easy, quick, nutritious addition to your favourite lunchtime salad or wrap. The hit of dietary fibre will help keep you feeling full all afternoon. For even more protein, add a small can of tuna or some cooked chicken or turkey.

Spread them, dip them Swap your regular mayo (loaded with fat) for some hummus (made from chickpeas) or white bean dip. Spread it on sandwiches or try it on veggie sticks.

Mash it up Swap your regular potato mash for white bean or chickpea mash. Higher in protein, dietary fibre and several nutrients, it's a win all round. Add spices, garlic, lemon zest and a little stock for a super-tasty chickpea version, or try white beans processed with ricotta, lemon and herbs for low-fat creamy mash.

Spice up your rice Next time you're cooking rice, toss in a handful of brown or green lentils.

Bake it Cooked legumes, such as white beans, black beans or even chickpeas, can be added to baked goods such as pancakes, muffins, biscuits, cakes or brownies. Try replacing some of the butter and flour with puréed beans. This will not only reduce the fat and kilojoule content, it will increase the nutritional value, too. Kids won't even know the legumes are there!

Replace some of the meat Swap half the meat in your regular curry, casserole, soup or stew for legumes. Not only will you add an extra serve of vegetables, dietary fibre and protein, you'll lower the overall cost.

Meat-free Monday Take it one step further and implement meat-free Monday. Legumes are the perfect addition to any plant-based meal – rich in protein, satisfying to eat and so versatile. Try chickpea burgers, kidney bean casserole or lentil bolognese for a twist on a family favourite.

AND ENVIRONMENTAL BENEFITS?

As well as being delicious and nutritious, legumes are good for the environment too! Legumes have a more efficient protein yield than livestock such as cattle, sheep or chicken. Overall, they are an environmentally friendly and sustainable source of dietary protein.

As legumes grow they develop root nodules that contain bacteria that can convert atmospheric nitrogen into ammonia; this, in turn, is used by the plant to produce protein. When the plant dies, residual plant nitrogen is returned to the soil for use by the next crop. For this very reason, legumes are often grown as a rotation crop, as they help enrich the soil.

TO SUM IT ALL UP

- Legumes are nutritious whole foods and are members of both the vegetable and high-protein food groups. A cup of legumes is considered two serves of vegetables or one serve of protein.
- Legumes are true superfoods, packed with plant protein and rich in dietary fibre, B vitamins, magnesium, zinc and iron.
- Legumes can be combined with grains in the daily diet to provide a source of complete protein.
- Canned legumes are handy and extremely versatile. Look for a brand with no or minimal added salt.
- Legumes can cause tummy discomfort for some people. To minimise symptoms, pre-soak dried beans, rinse them thoroughly after cooking, and introduce them to your diet gradually.
- Most of us do not eat nearly enough legumes. We should be trying to increase our intake, so that we're eating both more vegetables and more plant protein.
- Legumes are an environmentally friendly and sustainable source of dietary protein.

BUTTER BEAN, CHILLI AND
CORN FRITTERS WITH
CUCUMBER SALAD

(see recipe page 44)

**BAKED EGGS AND BEANS
WITH HUMMUS TOASTS**

(see recipe page 45)

BUTTER BEAN, CHILLI AND CORN FRITTERS
WITH CUCUMBER SALAD

Butter beans are a nutritious addition to veggie fritters: they're extremely low in fat, high in protein and rich in dietary fibre. They also add body and texture, which means you need only a little flour to bind the mixture.

Preparation time: 20 minutes
Cooking time: 30 minutes
Serves 4

1 tablespoon olive oil

400 g (14 oz/2 cups) fresh corn kernels (see tips)

1/2 red capsicum (pepper), diced

4 spring onions (scallions), thinly sliced

1 long green chilli, seeded and finely chopped

2 garlic cloves, crushed

400 g (14 oz) can butter beans, rinsed (see tips)

2 eggs

75 g (2³/4 oz/1/2 cup) wholemeal spelt flour

2 tablespoons chopped flat-leaf (Italian) parsley

Salad leaves, to serve (optional)

CUCUMBER SALAD

2 Lebanese (short) cucumbers

2 tablespoons natural yoghurt

1 tablespoon chopped flat-leaf (Italian) parsley

1 tablespoon chopped dill

1 tablespoon lemon juice

Heat 1 teaspoon of the oil in a large non-stick frying pan over medium heat and cook the corn, capsicum, spring onions and chilli, stirring, for 2 minutes or until just tender. Add the garlic and stir for 30 seconds. Transfer to a large bowl and leave to cool.

Mix the butter beans and eggs in a food processor until smooth. Add the flour and process until well combined. Add to the corn mixture, then stir in the parsley. Season with sea salt and black pepper.

Heat the remaining oil in a large non-stick frying pan over medium–high heat. Add 1/4 cup of mixture per fritter, cooking three at a time. Cook for 3 minutes each side or until golden and cooked through. Keep warm while you cook the rest, using a little more oil if necessary.

To make the cucumber salad, peel the cucumber into ribbons, stopping when you reach the seeds. Stir together the cucumber ribbons, yoghurt, parsley, dill and lemon juice.

Serve the hot fritters with the cucumber salad and salad leaves.

+ TIPS +

For a gluten-free version, replace the spelt flour with gluten-free plain (all-purpose) flour.

You'll need 2–3 cobs of corn for this recipe.

You can replace the butter beans with cannellini beans.

(pictured page 42)

BAKED EGGS AND BEANS
WITH HUMMUS TOASTS

*Eggs and beans provide a winning combo of protein and dietary fibre, guaranteed
to keep you full until lunchtime. You'll need a large non-stick frying pan with a lid
for this recipe.*

Preparation time: 20 minutes
Cooking time: 20 minutes
Serves 4

2 teaspoons olive oil

1 red onion, finely chopped

2 garlic cloves, crushed

1 long red chilli, seeded and
finely chopped

1 teaspoon paprika

1 teaspoon ground cumin

1/2 teaspoon dried oregano

400 g (14 oz) can cherry tomatoes
or diced tomatoes

255 g (9 oz/1^1/2 cups) cooked
red kidney beans (see tips)

4 eggs

30 g (1 oz) feta cheese, crumbled

4 slices rye or wholegrain bread
(see tips)

2 tablespoons hummus

Chopped flat-leaf (Italian) parsley,
to garnish

Heat the olive oil in a large non-stick frying pan over medium heat. Add the onion and cook, stirring, for 5 minutes or until softened. Add the garlic, chilli, paprika, cumin and oregano and cook, stirring, for 1 minute or until fragrant.

Stir in the tomatoes and 80 ml (2^1/2 fl oz/^{1}/3 cup) water. Add the beans and simmer for 10 minutes or until the sauce has thickened.

Make four holes in the sauce with a wooden spoon. Carefully crack an egg into each hole, then crumble the feta over the top. Cover the pan and simmer until the eggs are cooked to your liking (about 4 minutes for soft-poached).

Meanwhile, toast the bread and spread it with the hummus. Garnish the eggs with chopped parsley and serve with the hummus toasts.

✦ TIPS ✦

This recipe is gluten free if you use gluten-free bread.

You can replace the cooked kidney beans with 400 g (14 oz) canned beans, rinsed. Look for a brand with little or no added salt.

(pictured page 43)

CANNELLINI BEAN, TUNA AND CAPER DIP

Cannellini beans are high in protein and fibre, have a low GI and are virtually fat free. Their delicious creamy texture works perfectly in this dip. Serve this with veggie sticks for a super-healthy snack, or spread it over wholegrain crackers.

Preparation time: 10 minutes
Cooking time: None
Serves 6–8

400 g (14 oz) can cannellini beans, rinsed

185 g (6½ oz) can tuna in olive oil, drained, oil reserved

1 tablespoon lemon juice

1 tablespoon baby salted capers, rinsed and chopped

2 tablespoons chopped flat-leaf (Italian) parsley, plus extra to garnish

½ small red onion, very finely chopped

Olive oil, to garnish (optional)

Vegetables, such as snow peas (mangetout), carrots, radishes and asparagus, for dipping

Process the cannellini beans, tuna, 1 tablespoon of the reserved oil and the lemon juice in a food processor until almost smooth, adding a little extra oil if necessary.

Add the capers, parsley and most of the onion and pulse until combined, leaving some texture. Season to taste with black pepper.

Garnish with the remaining onion, extra parsley and a drizzle of olive oil. Serve with vegetables for dipping.

+ **TIP** +

This will keep in an airtight container in the fridge for 3 days.

PRAWN AND BLACK BEAN SOUP
WITH LIME

Black beans contain the winning combo of high protein and high fibre. Their distinctive black coating is also rich in anthocyanins – these pigments (also found in blueberries) have a powerful antioxidant effect that may help to prevent cancer and heart disease.

Preparation time: 20 minutes
Cooking time: 1 hour 20 minutes
Serves 4 as a light meal

165 g (5^3/$_4$ oz/^{3}/$_4$ cup) dried black beans, soaked overnight in cold water and drained (see tip)

2 teaspoons olive oil

1 red onion, finely chopped

2 celery stalks, diced

3 garlic cloves, crushed

1 chipotle pepper in adobo sauce, finely chopped

2 teaspoons paprika

1 teaspoon ground cumin

Pinch of cayenne pepper

2 tablespoons chopped coriander (cilantro) leaves

3 large vine-ripened tomatoes, diced

750 ml (26 fl oz/3 cups) home-made or low-salt vegetable or chicken stock

400 g (14 oz) peeled raw prawns (shrimp), tails intact

1 tablespoon lime juice, plus lime wedges to serve

Sliced avocado, to garnish

Put the black beans in a large saucepan, add enough cold water to cover them by 5 cm (2 inches) and bring to the boil. Reduce the heat to low and simmer for 45 minutes–1 hour until tender. Drain, rinse under cold running water and drain well.

Heat the olive oil in a large saucepan over medium heat. Add the onion and celery and cook, stirring, for 5 minutes or until softened. Add the garlic, chipotle, paprika, cumin, cayenne and coriander and cook, stirring, for 1 minute or until fragrant.

Add the tomatoes and cook for 1 minute, then add the stock and black beans and bring to the boil. Reduce the heat to low and simmer for 10 minutes. Add the prawns and simmer for 2–3 minutes or until the prawns are just cooked through. Add lime juice to taste and serve garnished with avocado, with lime wedges on the side.

+ TIP +

You can replace the cooked dried beans with 350 g (12 oz/2 cups) canned black beans, rinsed.

**MOROCCAN CARROT
AND CHICKPEA SALAD**

(see recipe page 52)

RAW BEETROOT AND LENTIL SALAD
WITH MUSTARD DRESSING
(see recipe page 53)

MOROCCAN CARROT AND CHICKPEA SALAD

This delicious salad is just the thing for when you're asked to take a plate to a barbecue – it's quick and easy and can even be made a day in advance. To turn this into a more substantial meal, add a handful of chopped nuts or a little crumbled feta.

Preparation time: 20 minutes
Cooking time: None
Serves 4 as a side dish

1 1/2 tablespoons white balsamic vinegar

1 tablespoon extra virgin olive oil

2 teaspoons honey (see tips)

1 teaspoon ground cumin

1/2 teaspoon ground coriander

1/4 teaspoon ground cinnamon

300 g (10 1/2 oz/about 4) carrots, thinly sliced into rounds

400 g (14 oz) can chickpeas, rinsed (see tips)

2 celery stalks, diced

2 tablespoons chopped coriander (cilantro) leaves

2 tablespoons chopped flat-leaf (Italian) parsley

1 tablespoon currants

Mix the vinegar, olive oil, honey and spices in a large bowl, add the carrot and stir to coat. Leave for 5 minutes for the flavours to develop.

Stir in the chickpeas, celery, coriander, parsley and currants. Season to taste with sea salt and freshly ground black pepper.

+ TIPS +

For a vegan version, replace the honey with maple syrup, or just leave it out.

You can replace the canned chickpeas with 225 g (8 oz/1 1/2 cups) drained cooked chickpeas.

(pictured page 50)

RAW BEETROOT AND LENTIL SALAD
WITH MUSTARD DRESSING

I absolutely love raw beetroot in salads, especially when it's teamed with nutty puy lentils and lots of chopped herbs for freshness. Beetroot is a good source of folate and is rich in phytochemicals, which may help to lower the risk of heart disease. Serve this as a side salad or add some grilled chicken, tofu or lamb to turn it into a meal.

Preparation time: 15 minutes
Cooking time: 25 minutes
Serves 4

160 g (5¾ oz/¾ cup) puy lentils, rinsed

2 teaspoons olive oil

1 red onion, finely chopped

2 celery stalks, finely chopped

400 g (14 oz/about 3) beetroot (beets), coarsely grated (see tips)

1 tablespoon extra virgin olive oil

1 tablespoon balsamic vinegar

2 teaspoons wholegrain mustard

1 teaspoon honey (see tips)

2 tablespoons chopped flat-leaf (Italian) parsley

2 tablespoons chopped mint

Cook the lentils in a saucepan of boiling water for 20–25 minutes or until just tender. Refresh under cold running water and drain well.

Meanwhile, heat the olive oil in a large non-stick frying pan over medium heat. Add the onion and cook, stirring, for 5 minutes or until softened. Remove from the heat and add the lentils, celery and beetroot.

Whisk together the extra virgin olive oil, vinegar, mustard and honey. Pour the dressing over the lentil mixture, add the parsley and mint and toss gently. Season to taste with sea salt and freshly ground black pepper.

+ TIPS +

For a vegan version, replace the honey with maple syrup, or just leave it out.

When you're handling the beetroot, wear plastic gloves so your hands don't become stained.

This salad will keep in an airtight container in the refrigerator for up to 2 days.

(pictured pages 50–51)

ADZUKI BEAN, BROWN RICE AND EDAMAME SUSHI SALAD
WITH POACHED EGG

This salad is a sort of free-form vegetarian nori roll with all the goodness of adzuki beans and brown rice, topped off with a poached egg. Grains and legumes are made for each other because together they form a complete protein, which is especially important if you're following a vegetarian or vegan diet. I love using brown rice rather than white, not only for its nutritional advantages but because it has so much more flavour and texture. Serve the poached egg hot or at room temperature.

Preparation time: 20 minutes
Cooking time: 25 minutes
Serves 4

220 g (7³/4 oz/1 cup) brown rice

2 tablespoons sushi seasoning

1 tablespoon low-salt tamari

250 g (9 oz) fresh or frozen edamame

400 g (14 oz) can adzuki beans, rinsed

1 large carrot, grated

1 Lebanese (short) cucumber, seeded and diced

1 avocado, diced (see tip)

4 spring onions (scallions), thinly sliced

4 eggs, poached

1 nori sheet, cut into thin strips

2 teaspoons sesame seeds, lightly toasted

Cook the brown rice in a large saucepan of boiling water for 20–25 minutes or until just tender. Drain well, transfer to a large bowl, stir in the sushi seasoning and tamari and leave to cool.

Meanwhile, cook the edamame in a steamer over a saucepan of simmering water for 2 minutes or until bright green. Refresh under cold water, drain and remove the beans from the pods.

Gently stir the edamame beans, adzuki beans, carrot, cucumber, avocado and spring onions into the rice mixture.

Serve each salad topped with a poached egg, garnished with nori strips and toasted sesame seeds.

+ TIP +

Squeeze a little lemon juice over the avocado as soon as you dice it to prevent discolouring.

SPELT PASTA AND CHICKPEAS
WITH ITALIAN SAUSAGE AND ROCKET

Chickpeas have a nutty taste that's perfect with wholegrain pasta such as spelt. Choose good-quality pork and fennel sausages for this dish, but remember that the chickpeas mean you only need a small amount of sausage, which reduces the serving of meat and the cost of the meal. They increase the fibre content, too.

Preparation time: 15 minutes
Cooking time: 15 minutes
Serves 4

250 g (9 oz) wholegrain pasta (such as wholegrain spelt; see tips)

1 tablespoon olive oil

1 red onion, finely chopped

1 small fennel bulb, finely chopped

2 garlic cloves, crushed

Finely grated zest of 1 lemon

1/2 teaspoon chilli flakes

250 g (9 oz/about 2) Italian pork and fennel sausages, removed from casings and crumbled (see tips)

400 g (14 oz) can chickpeas, drained and rinsed (see tips)

80 ml (2 1/2 fl oz/1/3 cup) home-made or low-salt chicken stock (see tips)

75 g (2 3/4 oz/1 3/4 cups) rocket (arugula) leaves

Grated parmesan cheese, to serve (optional)

Cook the pasta in lightly salted boiling water until al dente. Drain well and return to the saucepan.

Meanwhile, heat the olive oil in a large non-stick frying pan over medium heat. Add the onion and fennel and cook, stirring, for 5–6 minutes or until softened. Add the garlic, lemon zest and chilli and cook, stirring, for 1 minute or until fragrant.

Increase the heat to medium–high. Add the sausage meat and cook, breaking up the meat with a wooden spoon, for 3–4 minutes or until golden. Add the chickpeas and stock and simmer for 2 minutes or until heated through and slightly reduced.

Toss the sausage mixture and rocket with the pasta. Season to taste with sea salt and freshly ground black pepper. Serve with parmesan.

+ TIPS +

For a gluten-free version, use gluten-free pasta, sausages and stock.

You can replace the canned chickpeas with 225 g (8 oz/1 1/2 cups) drained cooked chickpeas.

GRILLED PORK
WITH BROAD BEAN, PEA AND APPLE SALAD

The legumes in this dish – broad beans and green peas – are served fresh. They have a short season, especially the broad beans, but you can substitute frozen legumes at any time of year and still enjoy the nutritional benefits. The beans and peas are both rich in soluble fibre, which has been linked to reduced blood cholesterol, and vitamin A, which is essential for good eye health.

Preparation time: 25 minutes
Cooking time: 10 minutes
Serves 4

2 teaspoons fennel seeds, crushed

2 teaspoons finely grated lemon zest

1/2 teaspoon sea salt

4 x 150 g (51/2 oz) French-trimmed pork loin cutlets

2 teaspoons extra virgin olive oil, plus extra for brushing

350 g (12 oz/2 cups) podded fresh or frozen broad beans, peeled (see tip)

210 g (71/2 oz/11/2 cups) podded fresh or frozen green peas

1 red apple, thinly sliced

4 small radishes, thinly sliced

2 teaspoons lemon juice, plus lemon wedges (optional) to serve

1 handful herbs, such as flat-leaf (Italian) parsley leaves and mint leaves

50 g (13/4 oz) snow pea (mangetout) tendrils or baby English spinach leaves

Combine the fennel seeds, lemon zest and salt and sprinkle evenly over both sides of the pork cutlets. Brush the pork with oil.

Heat a large chargrill pan over medium heat and cook the pork for 4–5 minutes each side or until lightly charred and cooked to your liking. Transfer to a plate, cover loosely with foil and leave to rest for 3 minutes.

Meanwhile, cook the broad beans and peas in boiling water for 2 minutes or until just tender. Refresh under cold water and drain well.

Toss together the apple, radish, lemon juice and olive oil in a large bowl. Add the broad beans, peas, herbs and snow pea tendrils and toss again. Season to taste with sea salt and freshly ground black pepper.

Serve the pork cutlets with the salad and a wedge of lemon.

✦ TIP ✦

An easy way to peel frozen broad beans is to put them in a large bowl of cold water and leave for 5 minutes to thaw. They can then be peeled.

MEXICAN SLOW-COOKED PINTO BEANS

Pinto beans, like all legumes, have a low GI and are packed with dietary fibre, which has the effect of stabilising blood sugar levels. Extremely nutritious, they are rich in potassium, which assists healthy heart function, and in folate and magnesium. Serve this dish with brown rice or quinoa to make a complete protein.

Preparation time: 15 minutes
Cooking time: 2 hours 10 minutes
Serves 4–6

2 teaspoons olive oil

1 large onion, finely chopped

2 celery stalks, diced

100 g (3^1/$_2$ oz) speck, diced

1 red capsicum (pepper), diced

2 garlic cloves, crushed

2 long red chillies, seeded
and finely chopped

1 teaspoon smoked paprika

1 teaspoon ground cumin

1 teaspoon ground coriander

400 g (14 oz) can diced tomatoes

200 g (7 oz/1 cup) dried pinto beans,
soaked overnight in cold water
and drained

Preheat the oven to 160°C (315°F). Heat the oil in a large flameproof casserole dish over medium heat. Add the onion, celery and speck and cook, stirring, for 5 minutes or until softened. Add the capsicum, garlic, chilli and spices and cook, stirring, for 1 minute or until fragrant.

Add the tomatoes, beans and 375 ml (13 fl oz/1^1/$_2$ cups) water and bring to the boil. Cover, transfer to the oven and cook for 2 hours or until the beans are very tender. Serve hot.

+ TIPS +

For a vegan version, leave out the speck.

The slow-cooked beans can be frozen in airtight containers for up to 2 months.

BORLOTTI BEAN, PUMPKIN AND COCONUT CURRY

The creamy texture and rich flavour of borlotti beans makes them perfect for a vegetarian curry. High in fibre, they also make a complete protein when served with steamed brown rice or quinoa. Making your own curry paste takes only a few minutes and it's worth it, not only for the fresh flavour but so that you can skip the high sodium content of most commercial pastes.

Preparation time: 30 minutes
Cooking time: 1 hour
Serves 4

190 g (6³/4 oz/1 cup) dried borlotti beans, soaked overnight in cold water and drained

1 tablespoon macadamia or peanut oil

375 ml (13 fl oz/1¹/2 cups) home-made or low-salt vegetable stock (see tip)

250 ml (9 fl oz/1 cup) coconut milk

500 g (1 lb 2 oz) pumpkin (winter squash), cut into 2 cm (³/4 inch) cubes

150 g (5¹/2 oz) green beans, sliced

Lime juice, to taste

Coriander (cilantro) leaves, to garnish

CURRY PASTE

1 red onion, chopped

¹/4 cup coriander (cilantro) leaves

2 tablespoons chopped coriander (cilantro) root

1 lemongrass stem, chopped

2 long red chillies, seeded and chopped

2 garlic cloves, crushed

2 teaspoons finely grated ginger

1 teaspoon finely grated lime zest

Place the borlotti beans in a large saucepan, add cold water to cover the beans by 5 cm (2 inches) and bring to the boil. Reduce the heat to low and simmer for 45 minutes–1 hour or until tender. Drain well.

Meanwhile, to make the curry paste, process all the ingredients in a food processor until smooth.

Heat the oil in a large saucepan or wok over medium heat. Add the curry paste and cook, stirring, for 2 minutes or until fragrant. Stir in the stock and coconut milk and simmer for 10 minutes. Add the pumpkin and simmer, partially covered, for 10 minutes or until just tender. Add the borlotti beans and green beans and simmer for 3–4 minutes or until the green beans are just tender.

Season to taste with lime juice and sprinkle with coriander to serve.

+ **TIP** +
For a gluten-free version, use gluten-free stock.

CAROB, PEANUT BUTTER AND BANANA OAT BARS

Carob and peanuts are both legumes, with all the nutritional benefits the name implies. For flavour, you can't beat freshly ground peanut butter, which contains no added sugar or salt. It's available from most health-food shops and some delis.

Preparation time: 15 minutes
Cooking time: 20 minutes
Makes 20

200 g (7 oz/2 cups) rolled (porridge) oats
85 g (3 oz/1/2 cup) seedless raisins
85 g (3 oz/1/2 cup) small carob buttons
40 g (11/2 oz/1/4 cup) sunflower seeds
35 g (11/4 oz/1/2 cup) shredded coconut
1 teaspoon ground cinnamon
1 large ripe banana, mashed
1 egg
1 teaspoon natural vanilla extract
90 g (31/4 oz/1/3 cup) peanut butter
2 tablespoons maple syrup
1 tablespoon coconut oil

Preheat the oven to 180°C (350°F). Line a 16 x 26 cm (61/4 x 101/2 inch) baking tray, letting the baking paper hang over the sides of the tray so you can lift out the bars easily after baking.

Combine the oats, raisins, carob buttons, sunflower seeds, coconut and cinnamon in a large bowl.

Process the banana, egg and vanilla in a food processor until smooth.

Stir the peanut butter, maple syrup and coconut oil in a small saucepan over low heat until melted and smooth. Stir the peanut butter and banana mixtures into the oat mixture until well combined.

Press the mixture firmly into the tin and smooth the surface with the back of a spoon. Bake for 20 minutes or until golden. Cool completely before cutting into squares.

+ TIP +

These can be kept in an airtight container in the fridge for up to 1 week.

MEAT
& TOFU

MEAT & TOFU

Humans are omnivores: we eat both plants and animals. Meat has been our biggest, most efficient hit of 'complete protein' since we started hunting animals in prehistoric times, and the domestication of sheep, pigs and cattle around 9000 years ago has resulted in hugely increased meat consumption, but it isn't the only complete protein.

IS MEAT GOOD FOR US?

Meat is highly nutritious. All meat is a rich source of complete protein (it's 20–30 per cent protein), which means it contains all nine of the essential amino acids our bodies need to get from food.

Meat can be broadly classified as red or white, depending on the concentration of myoglobin in the muscle fibre. Beef, veal, lamb, goat and usually pork are referred to as 'red meat', whereas chicken and turkey are 'white meat'. In general, poultry and fish contain approximately one-third as much iron as red meat. The iron found in red meat is much more easily absorbed by our bodies than iron from plant sources, which is why vegetarians need to be particularly vigilant about their iron intake.

As well as high quantities of protein, meat contains many nutrients:

- iron to produce haemoglobin and transport oxygen
- zinc for a healthy immune system, healthy growth and metabolic processes
- vitamin B_6 for metabolism of protein and carbohydrates and formation of red blood cells
- vitamin B_{12}, essential for red blood cells and DNA
- riboflavin, which assists adrenal function and is essential for energy production
- niacin, which also assists growth and is essential for energy production
- selenium, an antioxidant that helps protects cells

Meat's fat content varies from 5 per cent to 35 per cent, depending on the animal's species, breed, age, rearing and diet. The kilojoule content largely reflects the fat content. For good health, it makes sense to choose lean cuts of meat, trim off excess fat and remove the skin from chicken before cooking. Cooking methods also affect fat content: grilling, stir-frying and roasting on a rack (so the fat can drain away) are all healthier than pan-frying or deep-frying.

HOW MUCH MEAT SHOULD WE EAT?

All forms of meat are rich sources of protein. Dietary guidelines worldwide classify meat as part of the high-protein food group, which also includes fish, eggs, tofu, legumes and nuts. Most dietary guidelines (including Australia's) recommend that we consume one to three serves from this group each day, with a maximum of seven serves of fresh lean meat per week.

Some people choose not to eat meat (vegetarians) or any food derived from animals (vegans) and to get their protein from other sources. There's a host of reasons behind these choices, including ethical objections to the killing of animals for food, concerns about the way animals are treated, health concerns, environmental concerns and religious laws.

AND WHAT IS A SERVE OF MEAT?

It's not uncommon to see 350 g (12 oz) steaks on a pub menu. Yet a healthy size serve of meat, according to dietary guidelines, looks like this:

- 90–100 g (3–3 1/2 oz) lean red meat (raw weight)
- 1/2 cup lean minced (ground) meat
- 2 small lamb cutlets or slices of roast meat
- 1 piece of steak or lamb the size of a pack of cards
- 100 g (3–3 1/2 oz) lean chicken or turkey (raw weight)

That pub steak, then, is three to four serves of meat in just one sitting. Occasionally eating a serve larger than the recommended size is fine – as long as you keep the overall number of serves each week in check. For example, you might enjoy a 180 g (6¼ oz) steak, and that's quite okay if you eat it only every second day.

GRASS-FED VERSUS GRAIN-FED BEEF

You might have noticed the terms 'grain-fed' and 'grass-fed' on restaurant menus or at your local butcher, but what do they really mean, and is one kind of beef better than the other?

In Australia, cattle spend most of their life on pasture (grass), but what they are fed during the last three to six months before slaughter varies. Cattle left on pasture are referred to as 'grass-fed', and cattle fed an energy-rich diet in a feed lot are described as 'grain-fed'. Grain-fed cattle are usually classified as short-fed (60–100 days) or long-fed (150–300 days).

Most beef sold in supermarkets is short-grain-fed, as this allows the supermarket to provide a consistent product year-round, regardless of seasonal variations in pasture.

AND THE NUTRITIONAL DIFFERENCES?

In terms of both nutrition and taste, the differences between grain-fed and grass-fed beef vary depending on the breed, cut of meat, level of marbling (intramuscular fat), type of forage, length of grain feeding, and cooking method.

Grass-fed beef tends to be lower in overall fat than grain-fed beef. It gains points for significantly higher levels of omega-3 fatty acids and lower levels of omega-6 fatty acids than grain-fed beef. This ratio of omega-3 to omega-6 is linked to improved heart health.

Grass-fed beef has similar iron and zinc levels to grain-fed, but it comes out on top for vitamin A (beta-carotene) and vitamin E. The fat of grass-fed beef tends to be slightly yellow from the beta-carotene, whereas grain-fed beef has white fat.

Grass-fed beef tends to have a more distinctive flavour, and this flavour can vary seasonally depending on what forage is available to the cattle. Some people see this as a good thing, but others, including many chefs and supermarket buyers, see the inconsistency as a negative. Grain-fed beef has a more subtle, predictable flavour, and it can be more tender.

I prefer and love the flavour of grass-fed beef, but like most things, it comes down to personal preference.

WHAT ABOUT LAMB?

Lamb meat, like beef, can be grass-fed or grain-fed. Lambs are marketed when they reach a target weight and level of fatness. In Australia, lambs are reared with their mothers on pasture until they are weaned. If they are reared on high-quality pasture, they may be marketed at the point of weaning (these animals are known as sucker lambs). Otherwise, they can remain on pasture, where they often receive supplementary feed as well, or they can be reared more intensively on a high-energy diet in a feedlot until they reach the target specifications.

FREE-RANGE, ORGANIC, CERTIFIED ORGANIC? WHAT DOES IT ALL MEAN?

The terms 'free-range' and 'organic' get bandied around a lot in relation to chicken meat production. Trying to find out what they mean, and which is the better choice, can be confusing.

Most of the chicken meat sold in supermarkets is neither free-range nor organic, but barn-reared. Barn-reared chickens are kept enclosed in sheds all the time. Barn-reared chickens can be given antibiotics, whereas free-range and certified organic chickens cannot.

'Free-range' *should* refer to chickens that have access to outside forage areas during the day, but legislated definitions of the term – where they exist at all – vary. For example, 'free-range' chickens in the USA must have access to the outside, but this could consist of dirt or gravel – there is no requirement for grass. In Australia the term is not defined in legislation (only in voluntary codes, which vary a lot); in the EU countries it is defined and regulated strictly. For a guide to the various voluntary Australian standards and accreditation schemes, visit the Sustainable Table website at www.sustainabletable.org.au.

In Australia, organic production is more highly regulated than free-range production, but certification is still voluntary – so the key term to look for is 'certified organic'. To be certified organic, chickens must have access to outside forage during the day and meet other criteria in relation to their diet and the way they're managed. Certified organic chickens are also slaughtered later, at 65–80 days of age, than free-range and barn-reared chickens, which are killed at 35–55 days.

There's not much to stop a producer from selling chicken meat (or vegetables or fruit or anything else) at a local farmers' market and calling it 'organically grown' or 'organic'. It might well meet the required standards, but unless the product is labelled 'certified organic' and carries the logo of the certification body, you have to take it on trust. That said, if you do have a trusting relationship with a local grower, it's a win-win.

Nutritionally, there is little evidence of any difference between free-range and barn-reared chicken. Free-range and organic chickens are often said to taste better (I think they do) from getting a greater range of flavonoids in their diet. The other issue to consider, of course, is the ethical treatment of animals. Many people prefer to eat chicken that has not been reared in overcrowded sheds.

FREE-RANGE PORK

You might have seen pork labelled 'free-range' or 'sow stall free', but what does it mean?

'Free-range' means, loosely, that the sows (female pigs) are not kept in stalls but are reared in outdoor paddocks with their piglets and are provided with food, water and shelter.

'Outdoor-bred' or 'bred free-range' are piglets raised outdoors, free-range, with their mothers until weaning, at which point they are moved indoors.

More intensive systems include indoor individual or group pens with concrete or slatted floors, which often receive negative media attention, and deep litter housing, where groups of pigs of similar ages are kept in open-sided sheds with a floor of deep straw, sawdust or other dry matter.

Free-range pork tends to have a better flavour and texture as a result of the animals' access to green pasture. In addition, it's often produced from traditional or heirloom breeds which tend to be higher in fat and better flavoured than modern hybrid breeds.

AND THAT BACON SANDWICH?

Cured meats such as bacon and salami can be so delicious, but are they actually good for us? Processed meats are generally enriched with additives to protect or modify their flavour or colour, improve tenderness or shelf life. Common additives include:

- salt to enhance flavour, inhibit microbial growth and aid emulsification in foods such as sausages
- sodium nitrate and potassium nitrite to stabilise colour and flavour and inhibit micro-organisms
- phosphates to improve emulsifying abilities, limit flavour loss and reduce microbial growth
- sweeteners, such as sugar and corn syrup
- flavourings and flavour enhancers, such as monosodium glutamate (MSG)

Obviously, once a meat is processed, its nutritional integrity and health benefits are compromised. The addition of additives generally results in higher sodium levels, added sugar and a host of other possible artificial flavourings. So processed meat, such as that bacon sandwich, really should be considered an occasional food, rather than a regular part of the diet. Especially for children, who are more sensitive to the sodium and other potential additives.

SO WHY IS TOFU IN THIS CHAPTER?

Our bodies need protein to live and meat is a very efficient source of complete protein, but it isn't the only one. Tofu is an extremely nutritious vegetarian source of complete protein (it's about 8 per cent protein) that can provide all nine of the essential amino acids we need from food.

Tofu is naturally gluten and cholesterol free and has a relatively low calorie count. It's rich in phytochemicals such as phyto-oestrogens and isoflavones, which are linked to health benefits including, famously, lessening the symptoms associated with menopause. Tofu is also high in several nutrients, including iron, calcium, magnesium, potassium and the B vitamins. Replacing some of your animal protein intake with soy protein such as tofu is also linked to improved heart health. So, there are plenty of reasons to swap meat for tofu in your next stir-fry.

AND WHAT IS TOFU?

Tofu, also known as bean curd, is derived from soy beans. It's made by coagulating soy milk, then pressing the resulting curds into soft white blocks, in much the same way that cheese is made. The texture is determined by how much whey is pressed out:

- silken: has a soft, silky texture, best used in desserts or blended in sauces or smoothies for a protein hit
- soft: great for steaming, or in soups or casseroles
- firm: keeps its shape during cooking, so works well in curries and stir-fries
- extra-firm: ideal to grill or barbecue

HOW MUCH TOFU SHOULD WE EAT?

Tofu is classified as a high-protein food and therefore grouped with meat, poultry, fish, eggs, legumes and nuts. Most world dietary guidelines (including Australia's) recommend that we consume one to three serves from this food group each day.

WHAT IS A SERVE OF TOFU?

Under the Australian dietary guidelines, a serve is 170 g (6 oz). In terms of protein, it's the equivalent of 65 g (2 1/4 oz) lean red meat, 80 g (2 3/4 oz) poultry or 100 g (3 1/2 oz) fish (cooked weights).

AND HOW DO VEGETARIANS GET THEIR IRON?

It's true that the iron we get from meat (haem iron) is the type most easily absorbed by our bodies. There is non-haem iron in tofu and in leafy green vegetables, whole grains, dried fruits and legumes, but it's not as efficiently absorbed, and vegetarians and vegans need to keep an eye on their intake.

Combining vitamin C with non-haem iron helps the body absorb it. So, a glass of fresh orange juice with a meal, or adding some vitamin C-rich red, orange or yellow foods (capsicums are my favourites here) to a green stir-fry will work wonders. Interestingly, you'll also absorb more iron from cooked green leafy vegetables or broccoli than from eating them raw.

TO SUM IT ALL UP

- All forms of meat are rich sources of protein and other essential nutrients, including iron, zinc and B vitamins. Choose lean cuts or trim off the fat.
- Grass-fed beef is slightly better than grain-fed beef in nutritional terms and has a distinctive flavour. Grain-fed beef can be more tender.
- When you're buying chicken or pork, read the labels and look for standards that meet your requirements if you want to choose free-range or organic.
- Processed meats such as bacon contain a lot of salt and other additives, so eat them only in moderation.
- Tofu is an excellent source of plant protein and other nutrients and can be substituted for meat in several meals. It is also rich in phytochemicals, which have various health benefits.

**TURKEY LARB IN COS
LETTUCE CUPS**
(see recipe page 72)

STICKY TOFU STEAKS
WITH ASIAN SLAW
(see recipe page 73)

TURKEY LARB
IN COS LETTUCE CUPS

Turkey breast is protein-rich and extremely lean; it contains less saturated fat than beef, pork or chicken. Serve this dish with a simple side salad, such as sliced cucumber and vine-ripened tomato.

Preparation time: 20 minutes
Cooking time: 15 minutes
Serves 4

2 teaspoons macadamia or peanut oil

1 tablespoon brown rice

400 g (14 oz) minced (ground) turkey breast (see tip)

1 stem lemongrass, white part only, finely chopped

1 long red chilli, seeded and finely chopped

2 garlic cloves, crushed

1 tablespoon chopped coriander (cilantro) root

2 teaspoons finely grated ginger

200 g (7 oz) green beans, thinly sliced

1 tablespoon lime juice

1 tablespoon fish sauce

2 teaspoons brown or palm sugar

1/2 cup mint leaves

1/2 cup coriander (cilantro) leaves

1/2 small red onion, thinly sliced

175 g (6 oz/1 1/2 cups) bean sprouts, trimmed

8 cos (romaine) lettuce leaves

Heat 1 teaspoon of the oil in a large wok or non-stick frying pan over medium heat and stir-fry the rice for 1 minute or until golden brown and aromatic. Cool, then finely crush with a mortar and pestle.

Add the remaining oil to the wok over high heat. Add the turkey and stir-fry, breaking up the meat, for 7 minutes or until browned. Add the lemongrass, chilli, garlic, coriander root and ginger and stir-fry for 1 minute or until aromatic. Add the green beans and stir-fry for 2 minutes or until almost tender.

Stir in the lime juice, fish sauce and sugar. Remove from the heat and cool slightly then stir in the ground rice, herbs, onion and bean sprouts.

Spoon into lettuce cups to serve.

✦ TIP ✦
Minced (ground) pork or chicken work well in place of turkey.

(pictured page 70)

STICKY TOFU STEAKS
WITH ASIAN SLAW

Like steak, firm tofu is delicious marinated and ideal for grilling. Making your own marinade takes virtually no more time than choosing a commercially made sauce, and the result is delicious, without colourings, artificial flavours or MSG.

Preparation time: 20 minutes,
  plus 1 hour marinating
Cooking time: 5 minutes
Serves 4

1¹/₂ tablespoons honey (see tips)

1¹/₂ tablespoons low-salt tamari
(see tips)

2 teaspoons finely grated ginger

1 garlic clove, crushed

500 g (1 lb 2 oz) firm tofu, drained,
cut into 1 cm- (¹/₂ inch-) thick steaks

Olive oil spray

ASIAN SLAW

250 g (9 oz) bok choy (pak choy),
shredded

150 g (5¹/₂ oz) snow peas (mangetout),
shredded

1 red capsicum (pepper), thinly sliced

¹/₂ small Chinese cabbage (wong bok),
shredded

¹/₄ cup mint leaves

2 tablespoons slivered almonds,
toasted

1 tablespoon lime juice

1 tablespoon low-salt tamari (see tips)

2 teaspoons honey or brown sugar

1 long red chilli, seeded and
finely chopped

Combine the honey, tamari, ginger and garlic in a glass or ceramic dish. Add the tofu and gently turn to coat. Cover and marinate in the fridge for at least 1 hour.

Meanwhile, for the Asian slaw, combine the vegetables, mint and almonds in a large bowl. Whisk together the lime juice, tamari, honey and chilli. Add to the vegetables and gently toss.

Preheat a chargrill pan or barbecue to medium–high and spray with oil. Lift the tofu out of the marinade and grill for 2 minutes each side or until golden and lightly charred, brushing with marinade as it cooks.

Serve the tofu steaks hot with the Asian slaw.

+ TIPS +

For a vegan version, replace the honey in the marinade with rice malt syrup or maple syrup.

For a gluten-free version, use gluten-free tamari.

(pictured page 71)

TOFU AND VEGETABLE CURRY
WITH RAITA

Tofu is a rich source of complete vegetarian protein: it contains all the essential amino acids and is rich in phytonutrients, which have disease-fighting properties. For curries, firm tofu works best because it retains its shape and absorbs the flavours of the spices. Finely chopped macadamia nuts enrich and thicken the sauce.

Preparation time: 20 minutes
Cooking time: 30 minutes
Serves 4

1 tablespoon macadamia or peanut oil

350 g (12 oz) firm tofu, cut into 2 cm (3/4 inch) cubes

1 eggplant (aubergine), cut into 3 cm (11/4 inch) cubes

1 onion, finely chopped

2 long red chillies, seeded and finely chopped

3 garlic cloves, crushed

2 teaspoons grated ginger

1 teaspoon cumin seeds

2 teaspoons ground coriander

1 teaspoon paprika

4 vine-ripened tomatoes, chopped

375 ml (13 fl oz/11/2 cups) home-made or low-salt vegetable stock (see tips)

2 large carrots, sliced into rounds

150 g (51/2 oz) green beans, sliced

2 tablespoons macadamia nuts, finely chopped

Raita, to serve (see tips)

Steamed quinoa or brown rice, to serve

Heat 1 teaspoon of the oil in a large wok or non-stick frying pan over high heat. Add the tofu and stir-fry for 2–3 minutes or until golden. Remove the tofu, add 2 more teaspoons oil to the wok and stir-fry the eggplant for 2 minutes or until golden. Remove the eggplant.

Reduce the heat to medium, add the remaining oil and stir-fry the onion for 3 minutes until light golden. Add the chilli, garlic, ginger and spices and stir-fry for 1 minute. Add the tomatoes and stock, bring to the boil, reduce the heat, cover and simmer for 5 minutes. Add the carrots, cover and simmer, stirring occasionally, for 10 minutes.

Return the tofu and eggplant to the wok with the green beans. Simmer for 2–3 minutes until the beans are just tender. Stir in the macadamias.

Serve the curry with raita and steamed quinoa or brown rice.

✦ TIPS ✦

For a gluten-free version, use gluten-free stock.

To make your own raita, combine 260 g (91/4 oz/1 cup) natural yoghurt, 1 grated Lebanese (short) cucumber, 2 tablespoons chopped mint, 1 crushed garlic clove and a squeeze of lemon juice.

SLOW-COOKED LAMB
SHOULDER WITH CAPONATA
(see recipe page 78)

LAMB LOIN ROAST ON
WHITE BEAN MASH WITH
ZUCCHINI SALAD

(see recipe page 79)

SLOW-COOKED LAMB SHOULDER
WITH CAPONATA

Lamb shoulder lends itself beautifully to slow cooking, becoming rich and meltingly tender. It's high in fat, so trim away as much visible fat as you can before cooking – the flavour will still be amazing. I like to serve this dish with loads of steamed greens to balance the richness of the meat.

Preparation time: 20 minutes
Cooking time: 2 hours 45 minutes
Serves 6

1 tablespoon dijon mustard

2 tablespoons balsamic vinegar

1 tablespoon coarsely chopped rosemary

1.2 kg (2 lb 11 oz) boneless lamb shoulder, excess fat trimmed

1 large eggplant (aubergine), cut into 1.5 cm (5/8 inch) dice

1 large red onion, cut into 1.5 cm (1/2 inch) dice

Olive oil spray

400 g (14 oz) grape tomatoes, halved

1/2 cup basil leaves, torn

2 tablespoons pine nuts, toasted

2 tablespoons currants

1 tablespoon salted baby capers, rinsed and chopped

2 teaspoons extra virgin olive oil

Steamed greens, to serve

Preheat the oven to 220°C (425°F). Mix together the mustard and 1 tablespoon of the vinegar to make a glaze. Place the lamb in a roasting tin, brush evenly with the mustard glaze and sprinkle with rosemary. Roast for 15 minutes or until browned.

Reduce the oven to 160°C (315°F). Place a large piece of baking paper over the lamb, tucking the edges under, then cover the whole tin with a piece of foil. Return to the oven and roast for 2 1/2 hours or until the lamb is so tender that it can be shredded with a fork. Brush the lamb with any remaining glaze and leave to cool slightly.

Meanwhile, place the eggplant and onion on a large tray lined with baking paper and spray with olive oil. Roast for 15 minutes. Add the tomatoes and roast for 10–15 minutes or until the eggplant is golden and tender and the tomatoes are wilted. Transfer to a large bowl and add the basil, pine nuts, currants, capers, olive oil and remaining vinegar. Season to taste with sea salt and freshly ground black pepper.

Coarsely shred the lamb and serve hot with the caponata and steamed greens.

(pictured page 76)

LAMB LOIN ROAST
ON WHITE BEAN MASH WITH ZUCCHINI SALAD

Boneless lamb loin makes a delicious mini roast, especially when it's served with white bean mash – a creamy, fibre-packed alternative to mashed potato.

Preparation time: 30 minutes
Cooking time: 20 minutes
Serves 4

50 g (1³/4 oz) roasted red capsicum (pepper), diced

40 g (1¹/2 oz) baby English spinach leaves, chopped

1 tablespoon chopped oregano

1 tablespoon pine nuts, toasted

500 g (1 lb 2 oz) lamb loin roast

1 teaspoon olive oil

WHITE BEAN MASH

1 teaspoon olive oil

1 garlic clove, crushed

1 teaspoon finely grated lemon zest

2 x 400 g (14 oz) tins cannellini beans, rinsed

125 ml (4 fl oz/¹/2 cup) home-made or low-salt chicken stock

1 tablespoon lemon juice, or to taste

ZUCCHINI SALAD

1 tablespoon olive oil

1 tablespoon lemon juice

1 teaspoon finely grated lemon zest

1 teaspoon dijon mustard

3 large zucchini (courgettes)

1 tablespoon each chopped oregano and snipped chives

Preheat the oven to 200°C (400°F). Mix together the capsicum, spinach, oregano and pine nuts to make a stuffing.

Remove any string from the lamb and unroll the meat. Spread the stuffing between the two long sections of the loin, then re-roll, keeping the skin and fat on the outside. Secure at intervals with kitchen string and brush the lamb with olive oil.

Heat a large non-stick frying pan over high heat. Add the lamb and cook for 1–2 minutes each side or until browned. Transfer to a roasting tin and roast until cooked to your liking (20 minutes for medium). Remove from the oven, cover loosely with foil and leave to rest for 10 minutes.

Meanwhile, for the white bean mash, heat the olive oil in a saucepan over medium heat. Add the garlic and lemon zest and cook, stirring, for 1 minute or until fragrant. Add the cannellini beans and stock and simmer for 2–3 minutes or until the liquid is reduced by half. Transfer the bean mixture to a food processor and mix until smooth. Add lemon juice to taste and season with sea salt and freshly ground black pepper. Return to a saucepan and stir over medium heat until warmed through.

For the zucchini salad, whisk the olive oil, lemon juice, lemon zest and mustard in a large bowl. Cut the zucchini into spaghetti-like strands using a spiraliser, or peel it into ribbons with a vegetable peeler. Add the zucchini and herbs to the bowl and gently toss with the dressing. Season to taste with sea salt.

Thickly slice the lamb and serve with the white bean mash and zucchini salad.

(pictured page 77)

DUKKAH PORK
WITH ROASTED APPLE AND BEETROOT SALAD

Spice blends such as dukkah are a great way to add lots of flavour to grilled or roasted meat or tofu. The spice 'seasoning' blends available in supermarkets, however, tend to be high in sodium and other additives, so do check the label or, even better, make your own (see tips).

Preparation time: 15 minutes
Cooking time: 30 minutes
Serves 4

600 g (1 lb 5 oz/2 bunches) baby beetroot (beets), scrubbed, leaves reserved

3 red apples, cored and cut into wedges

Olive oil spray

1¹/₂ tablespoons balsamic vinegar

2 teaspoons thyme leaves

4 x 100 g (3¹/₂ oz) pork loin steaks

1 tablespoon olive oil

2 tablespoons dukkah (see tips)

100 g (3¹/₂ oz) treviso radicchio, leaves torn (see tips)

50 g (1³/₄ oz/1 cup) baby English spinach leaves or baby kale

Preheat the oven to 200°C (400°F) and line a large baking tray with baking paper. Cut the beetroot into halves or quarters and arrange on the tray along with the apple wedges. Spray with olive oil, drizzle with 2 teaspoons of the vinegar and sprinkle with thyme. Roast for 30 minutes or until the beetroot are tender and the apples are golden.

Meanwhile, brush the pork with 1 teaspoon of the olive oil and sprinkle both sides with dukkah. Heat a large non-stick frying pan over medium heat. Add the pork and cook for 3–4 minutes each side or until browned and cooked to your liking. Remove, cover loosely with foil and set aside to rest for 5 minutes. Thickly slice.

Combine the radicchio and spinach in a large bowl. Add the beetroot, apple, remaining vinegar and remaining olive oil and toss to combine. Serve the pork with the roasted apple and beetroot salad.

✦ TIPS ✦

To make your own dukkah, lightly toast ¹/₄ cup pistachio nuts or almonds, 1 tablespoon sesame seeds, 2 teaspoons cumin seeds and 2 teaspoons coriander seeds. Pound with 1 teaspoon sea salt in a mortar and pestle until finely ground. This makes more than you'll need for the pork, but the remainder will keep for a month in an airtight container.

Treviso radicchio has elongated leaves and tends to have a milder flavour than the round variety.

BURGER WITHOUT THE BUN

I love a good burger, but I always think of the bun as a filler – I'd rather just eat the good stuff. This version of a burger skips the bread and is served with a tangy pickled cucumber salad, fresh tomato salsa and roasted sweet potato instead of chips – delicious, and good for you, too!

Preparation time: 25 minutes
Cooking time: 25 minutes
Serves 4

500 g (1 lb 2 oz) sweet potato, cut into rounds 5 mm (1/4 inch) thick

Olive oil spray

400 g (14 oz) minced (ground) pork and veal mixture (see tips)

1 small zucchini (courgette), grated

1/2 red onion, finely grated

35 g (11/4 oz/1/4 cup) oat bran (see tips)

1 egg

2 teaspoons tamari (see tips)

2 teaspoons dijon mustard

1 baby cos (romaine) lettuce, torn

1/2 avocado, thinly sliced

PICKLED CUCUMBER SALAD

2 tablespoons rice vinegar

2 teaspoons caster (superfine) sugar

2 cucumbers, cut into ribbons

1 red onion, thinly sliced

FRESH TOMATO SALSA

3 roma (plum) tomatoes, diced

1 tablespoon chopped flat-leaf (Italian) parsley

1/4 teaspoon chilli flakes, or to taste

Preheat the oven to 200°C (400°F). Line a large baking tray with baking paper. Place the sweet potato on the tray and spray lightly with olive oil. Roast for 25 minutes, or until golden and tender, turning once.

Combine the minced pork and veal, zucchini, onion, oat bran, egg, tamari and mustard and season with sea salt and freshly ground black pepper. Mix with your hands until well combined. Form into 4 patties, place on a baking tray, cover and refrigerate for 10 minutes.

For the pickled cucumber salad, combine the vinegar, sugar and a large pinch of salt in a large bowl. Add the cucumber and onion and toss to combine. Set aside for 10 minutes to pickle.

For the fresh tomato salsa, combine the tomato, parsley and chilli. Season to taste.

Preheat a chargrill pan over medium–high heat and spray with oil. Cook the patties for 4–5 minutes each side or until lightly charred and cooked through. (Alternatively, pan-fry them for 4 minutes each side.)

Serve the roasted sweet potato rounds topped with burger patties and fresh tomato salsa, with lettuce, avocado and pickled cucumber salad.

+ TIPS +

For a gluten-free version, replace the oat bran with gluten-free breadcrumbs and use gluten-free tamari.

You can replace the minced pork and veal with beef.

SPICE-RUBBED ROAST CHICKEN
STUFFED WITH HARISSA AND KALE COUSCOUS

Nothing beats a home-made roast chicken, especially when it's been rubbed with a fragrant Middle Eastern spice mix. Wholemeal couscous is higher in fibre than regular couscous and it has a delicious nutty flavour. You could use cracked wheat or freekeh instead, or brown rice for a gluten-free version.

Preparation time: 25 minutes
Cooking time: 1 hour 20 minutes
Serves 4

65 g (2¼ oz/⅓ cup) wholemeal couscous

1 tablespoon olive oil

1 red onion, finely chopped

2 garlic cloves, crushed

2 teaspoons harissa

100 g (3½ oz) kale, chopped

1 preserved lemon quarter, rinsed, flesh and pith removed, zest finely chopped

2 tablespoons chopped flat-leaf (Italian) parsley

1 teaspoon cumin seeds

1 teaspoon coriander seeds

¼ teaspoon ground cinnamon

1.6 kg (3 lb 8 oz) free-range chicken, cavity rinsed and patted dry

To make the stuffing, place the couscous in a heatproof bowl. Add 80 ml (2½ fl oz/⅓ cup) boiling water, cover with plastic wrap and set aside for 3–4 minutes to steam. Fluff the grains with a fork.

Heat 2 teaspoons of the oil in a large non-stick frying pan over medium heat. Add the onion and cook, stirring, for 5 minutes or until softened. Add the garlic and harissa and cook, stirring, for 30 seconds or until aromatic. Add the kale and cook, stirring, for 1–2 minutes or until wilted. Stir in the couscous, preserved lemon and parsley. Remove from the heat and cool completely.

Stir the cumin and coriander seeds in a small frying pan over low heat for 2 minutes. Transfer to a mortar and pestle, cool, then add the cinnamon and a large pinch of salt and pound until finely ground.

Preheat the oven to 220°C (425°F). Spoon the couscous mixture into the chicken cavity. Tie the legs together with kitchen string and put, breast side up, in a large roasting dish. Rub with the remaining oil, then sprinkle with the spice mixture and rub into the chicken skin.

Roast the chicken for 20 minutes, then reduce the oven to 190°C (375°F) and cook for 50 minutes or until the juices run clear when you pierce the thigh with a skewer. (If the chicken browns too quickly, cover with foil.) Cover with foil and rest for 10 minutes before carving.

HERB-CRUSTED VEAL RACK
WITH BRAISED BROAD BEANS AND PEAS

Veal racks are extremely lean, as well as being a good source of iron, protein and B vitamins, which are essential for energy and metabolism. Peas and broad beans, both legumes, are rich in dietary fibre and protein and a low-GI source of carbohydrate.

Preparation time: 20 minutes
Cooking time: 35 minutes
Serves 4

1/2 cup (lightly packed) flat-leaf (Italian) parsley leaves

40 g (1 1/2 oz) sourdough bread

40 g (1 1/2 oz/1/3 cup) walnut halves

2 tablespoons chopped sage

2 tablespoons olive oil

2 teaspoons dijon mustard

1 teaspoon honey

1 x 4-cutlet French-trimmed veal rack (about 600 g/1 lb 5 oz)

2 French shallots, finely chopped

2 garlic cloves, crushed

350 g (12 oz/2 cups) podded fresh or frozen broad beans (see tip)

280 g (10 oz/2 cups) podded fresh or frozen baby green peas (see tip)

80 ml (2 1/2 fl oz/1/3 cup) home-made or low-salt chicken stock

100 g (3 1/2 oz) trimmed silverbeet (Swiss chard), kale or English spinach, chopped

Preheat the oven to 200°C (400°F). Process the parsley, bread, walnuts and sage in a food processor until finely chopped. Add 1 tablespoon of the oil and the mustard and honey and pulse until well combined. Press the herb mixture evenly over the top of the veal rack.

Place the veal on a roasting rack over a baking tray and drizzle with 2 teaspoons of the oil. Roast to your liking (30–35 minutes, or an internal temperature of 65–70°C/150–160°F, for medium). Transfer to a large plate, cover loosely with foil and rest for 10 minutes.

Meanwhile, heat the remaining oil in a large non-stick frying pan over medium heat. Add the shallots and cook, stirring, for 5 minutes or until softened. Add the garlic and cook, stirring, for 30 seconds. Add the broad beans, peas and stock and simmer for 2 minutes. Add the silverbeet and cook, stirring, for 1–2 minutes or until just wilted. Season with sea salt and freshly ground black pepper.

Carve the veal into cutlets and serve with broad beans and peas.

✦ TIP ✦

When broad beans and peas are out of season, frozen ones will work perfectly well here.

GRILLED MAPLE AND MUSTARD CHICKEN
WITH FENNEL AND ASPARAGUS SALAD

Chicken breasts these days tend to be very large, weighing as much as 300 g (10½ oz) each – too much for one serving. I like to slice them through the middle to give two thin fillets per breast. This means they take only a few minutes to cook on each side and they don't dry out or become tough.

Preparation time: 15 minutes,
    plus 30 minutes marinating
Cooking time: 10 minutes
Serves 4

2 x 250 g (9 oz) chicken breast fillets

1 tablespoon dijon mustard

1 tablespoon maple syrup

Finely grated zest and juice of 1 lime

1 tablespoon olive oil

Olive oil spray

2 fennel bulbs, cut into slices 5 mm
(¼ inch) thick

2 bunches asparagus (about 16 spears)

200 g (7 oz) grape tomatoes, halved

100 g (3½ oz) rocket (arugula) leaves

2 teaspoons balsamic vinegar

Cut each chicken breast through the middle horizontally to give 4 thin fillets. Combine the mustard, maple syrup, lime zest, lime juice and 2 teaspoons of the olive oil in a shallow glass or ceramic dish. Add the chicken and turn to coat. Cover and set aside in the refrigerator to marinate for at least 30 minutes.

Preheat a chargrill pan or barbecue to medium–high. Drain excess marinade from the chicken and grill the chicken for 2–3 minutes each side or until lightly charred and cooked through. Transfer to a plate and keep warm. Spray the fennel and asparagus with olive oil and grill for 1–2 minutes each side or until just tender.

Combine the fennel, asparagus, tomatoes and rocket in a large bowl. Add the remaining olive oil and the vinegar and toss to combine. Serve the chicken with the fennel and asparagus salad.

MISO BEEF
WITH WOK-TOSSED SHIITAKES AND ASIAN GREENS

Lean beef cuts such as fillet (tenderloin) steak are not only an excellent source of protein, they are also rich in vitamins B_{12} and B_6 (which helps provide energy by breaking down protein and carbohydrates) and the minerals iron and zinc. Iron found in red meat is more easily used by the body than iron from plant sources.

Preparation time: 15 minutes,
    plus 1 hour marinating
Cooking time: 20 minutes
Serves 4

1 tablespoon miso paste

2 teaspoons finely grated ginger

1¹/₂ tablespoons tamari

1¹/₂ tablespoons mirin

3 teaspoons macadamia or peanut oil

500 g (1 lb 2 oz) beef eye fillet (tenderloin), trimmed

100 g (3¹/₂ oz) fresh shiitake mushrooms

6 spring onions (scallions), cut into batons

2 garlic cloves, thinly sliced

180 g (6¹/₄ oz) broccolini, chopped

250 g (9 oz) gai larn (Chinese broccoli), cut into 6 cm (2¹/₄ inch) lengths

Combine the miso paste, ginger, 1 tablespoon of the tamari and 1 tablespoon of the mirin in a glass or ceramic dish.

Heat 1 teaspoon of the oil in a non-stick frying pan over medium–high heat, add the beef and cook, turning, for 1 minute each side or until browned. Transfer the beef to the dish with the marinade, turn to coat, and cool completely. Cover and marinate in the refrigerator for at least 1 hour.

Preheat the oven to 200°C (400°F). Put a rack over a baking tray lined with baking paper. Put the beef on the rack and brush with marinade. Roast for 15–20 minutes for medium, or until cooked to your liking. Transfer to a plate, cover loosely with foil and rest for 10 minutes.

Meanwhile, heat the remaining oil in a large wok or non-stick frying pan over high heat. Add the shiitakes and spring onions and stir-fry for 1–2 minutes or until golden. Add the garlic and stir-fry for 30 seconds or until aromatic. Add the broccolini, stir-fry for 2 minutes, add the gai larn and stir-fry for 1–2 minutes or until just tender. Add the remaining tamari and mirin and toss together.

Slice the beef and serve with wok-tossed shiitakes and Asian greens.

EGGS, SEEDS & NUTS

EGGS, SEEDS & NUTS

Nuts and seeds are now being recognised as true superfoods, with unique health benefits and nutritional properties... but what exactly are they? These powerhouses are the inner edible parts of mature fruit, intended by nature to be the food source for a germinating plant, which is why they are a concentrated source of everything.

ARE SEEDS AND NUTS GOOD FOR US?

They sure are! These are highly nutritious and versatile foods in the kitchen. They also share the common link of being rich sources of vegetarian protein and are highly regarded for their rich levels of healthy monounsaturated and polyunsaturated fats (49–81 per cent). They tend to be high in dietary fibre, vitamin E, B vitamins, zinc, iron, potassium, calcium, magnesium and selenium.

A seed has a softer coat that can usually be eaten, while a nut often has a harder shell that has to be broken to release the edible portion. And, to make things really confusing, there is a lot of crossover between the correct botanical names and the common day terminology used. For example, some nuts are known as seeds and vice versa!

However they're termed, each nut and seed has its own unique (and impressive) nutritional profile:

- Almonds: rich in protein and with high levels of calcium for strong bones and teeth, and vitamin E for immunity and healthy skin
- Brazil nuts: rich in fibre and the powerful antioxidant selenium with its cancer-protecting properties
- Cashew nuts: a good source of plant iron and zinc (just a handful of cashews provides around 12 per cent of these two minerals). Zinc is important for healthy hair, skin and immunity
- Chestnuts: more like grains than nuts in nutritional terms, and often made into flour. Low in fat, high in low-GI carbohydrate and, eaten raw, rich in vitamin C
- Chia seeds: rich in protein; plant omega-3s for good heart health; dietary fibre; and calcium and manganese, both important for healthy bones

- Hazelnuts: rich in vitamin E, high in fibre for good gut health and a source of potassium, iron, zinc and folate, which is essential during pregnancy for prevention of neural tube defects
- Linseeds (flaxseeds): rich in omega-3 fatty acids, plus a good source of iron, B vitamins and antioxidants. Their high soluble fibre content makes them a good source of probiotics, for good gut health
- Macadamias: higher in monounsaturated fat (81 per cent) than any other nuts and rich in manganese and thiamin, one of the B vitamins essential for energy production
- Peanuts: not true nuts, but a good source of niacin, folate, fibre, vitamin E, magnesium, copper and zinc; importantly, unlike other nuts, peanuts are a source of complete protein
- Pecans: rich in fibre, protein, antioxidants and one of the few plant sources of omega-3 fatty acids, which are linked to improved heart health
- Pepitas (pumpkin seeds): a good source of protein, iron and B vitamins, which can be beneficial in times of stress
- Pistachios: a good source of plant iron, potassium and antioxidants, in particular resveratrol, the antioxidant with anti-cancer and anti-ageing properties (it's also found in red wine)
- Sesame seeds: rich in minerals such as copper and plant iron, both essential for healthy red blood cells
- Sunflower seeds: rich in vitamin E, important for immunity, healthy skin and eyes; also contains thiamin, selenium, fibre, copper, iron, zinc and folate
- Walnuts: a rich plant source of omega-3 fatty acids, as well as being a good source of potassium, both of which are linked to heart health

While seeds and nuts do have a high oil content, they are also low in saturated fats and rich in heart-friendly monounsaturated and polyunsaturated fatty acids, and many nuts are rich in omega-3 fatty acids. Diets rich in healthy fats are linked to health benefits such as well-regulated cholesterol levels and a reduced risk of stroke. It's well known that nuts and seeds are a valuable protein source in vegetarian diets (think 1970s nut roast). With the exception of peanuts, nuts do lack just one essential amino acid (lysine), so they aren't a complete protein. This can be easily overcome by pairing them with other protein sources such as legumes or grains throughout the day.

HOW MANY SERVES SHOULD WE EAT?

With a protein content of around nine to 26 per cent, seeds and nuts are classified in dietary guidelines worldwide as high-protein foods, which puts them in the same food group as meat, fish, poultry, eggs and legumes. It's recommended that we eat 1 serve of nut or seeds (or a combination) per day.

AND WHAT IS A SERVE?

One serve is 30 g (1 oz) or approximately one small handful of seeds or nuts, plus up to an additional 10 g (1/4 oz) per day as part of our 'healthy fat' food quota.

One serve of seeds/nuts per day can assist with weight management: the healthy fats provide satiety and help you feel full longer. The trick is to remember that nuts and seeds are an extremely energy- and nutrient-dense food and they also tend to be VERY moreish to eat, so keep your serving size appropriate.

ROASTED OR RAW?

Most of us assume that raw nuts are healthier, but there is negligible difference between raw and roasted. The main difference is that roasted nuts are slightly more concentrated in nutrients due to their lower water content, but on the flip side they are slightly lower in B vitamins, as these start to deteriorate when heated. Nuts can either be dry roasted, or roasted with oil. Dry-roasted nuts contain slightly less oil, but only by about 5 per cent, so it's not a deal breaker. Roasting also enhances the natural 'nut' flavour, which is why these could be considered yummier and nuttier than their raw counterparts.

The main issue with roasted nuts is the addition of salt or other flavourings. So, if roasted is your preference (and it's definitely mine!), choose dry roasted with no added salt, or roast them yourself.

NUT AND SEED BUTTERS

Nut butter used to automatically mean peanut butter, but there's now an abundance of nut and seed butters on the market, from almond to pistachio. Extremely nutritious, these can be spread on crackers, used as a dip for veggie sticks, or even added to smoothies for a creamy protein hit.

A true nut or seed butter should contain only nuts or seeds and that's it! Watch out for versions that contain added salt, sugar or oils (peanut butter is the main culprit here).

Making your own butters at home is extremely easy (and cost-effective) but you do need a high-powered processor or blender. If you can't make your own, look for peanut butter in a health food store where they freshly grind it, with absolutely no additives.

WHAT ABOUT EGGS? ARE THEY GOOD FOR US?

The egg is also an example of nature at its best: packed with nutrition and perfectly encased in a hard protective shell. Eggs would also have to be one of the most versatile foods around: not only a breakfast favourite, they are used in a multitude of savoury dishes and are essential in baking and desserts. Eggs are an inexpensive source of complete protein, containing all nine essential amino acids, and are also packed with other nutrients, including:

- Vitamin A, for healthy vision, skin and bones
- Vitamin D, essential for strong bones and teeth; it also aids calcium absorption
- Vitamin B_2, required for energy production and adrenal function; also for vision and skin health
- Vitamin B_6, essential for energy production and carbohydrate and protein metabolism
- Vitamin B_{12}, found only in animal products and required to make red blood cells
- Choline, for cell membranes and nerve tissue
- Zinc, essential for a healthy immune system, healthy growth and metabolic processes
- Iron, to produce haemoglobin and transport oxygen
- Lutein and zeaxanthin, both powerful antioxidants linked to eye health

SO HOW MANY EGGS SHOULD WE EAT?

Eggs belong to the high-protein food group, which also includes meat, fish, poultry, nuts, seeds and legumes. Most dietary guidelines recommend that we eat two or three serves of this group per day.

AND WHAT IS A SERVE OF EGGS?

A serve of eggs is defined in the guidelines as 2 large eggs (60 g/2¼ oz each). In terms of protein, 2 eggs is the equivalent of 90–100 g (3–3½ oz) raw lean red meat, 100 g (3½ oz) raw poultry, 115 g (4 oz) raw fish, 150 g (5½ oz) cooked legumes, 170 g (6 oz) tofu, or 30 g (1 oz) nuts or seeds.

YOLKS VERSUS WHITES

The yolk is definitely where the action is. It contains all the egg's fat content, slightly less than half its protein and most of its other nutrients, including vitamins A, D and E. (Egg yolks are one of the few foods that contain vitamin D.) In contrast, the white is virtually fat free and is actually about 90 per cent water and 10 per cent protein.

BUT WHAT ABOUT EGGS, FAT AND CHOLESTEROL?

In one large egg, more than half the kilojoules come from the fat content of the yolk (about 5 g per yolk). Of this, only around 30 per cent (or 2 g) is in the form of saturated fats. An egg yolk contains approximately 190 mg of cholesterol. Eggs have received some bad press in the past, with conflicting advice issued on whether we should restrict our consumption of eggs because of their cholesterol content. More recent studies indicate that blood cholesterol levels are not greatly influenced by the cholesterol we eat; rather, it is saturated fat and trans fats that are problematic. With only 2 g of saturated fat per egg and absolutely no trans fats, an egg a day shouldn't be an issue at all for most of us.

SUPER EGGS!

Omega-3 eggs are new to the market. Their yolks are lower in saturated fat and contain higher levels of healthy omega-3 fatty acids than conventional eggs. This is the result of feeding the chickens a diet rich in seeds that are packed with omega-3s.

HOW FRESH IS FRESH?

A fresh egg has a firm round yolk, and the white forms a thick gelatinous ring around the yolk. As the egg ages the yolk becomes flatter and the white becomes thinner and spreads further.

The larger end of the egg contains an air sac: in fresh eggs this is small, but as the egg ages the air sac increases in size. An age-old method of testing an egg for freshness is to place it in a bowl of water. A fresh egg will sink to the bottom and sit there horizontally. An egg that's not quite so fresh will sit vertically, and an egg that is well and truly past its use-by date will float. Not-so-fresh eggs are good for hard-boiling, because the larger air sac makes them easier to peel.

To maximise the shelf life of eggs, store them in their carton in the fridge.

WHAT ABOUT FREE-RANGE AND ORGANIC EGGS?

With free range, barn-laid and cage eggs on the market, what exactly is what, and which is the most nutritious choice? The term 'free-range' is generally taken to mean that hens have ready access to areas outside the barn during the day to forage and display natural behaviours such as scratching, flapping their wings and dust bathing. However, 'free-range' is not defined in legislation in all countries and nor is the amount of space a hen should have in which to range. Among the egg producers who undergo voluntary accreditation as free-range producers in Australia, for example, acceptable densities range from 750 to 10,000 hens per hectare, and some producers want this increased to 20,000 birds per hectare.

Certified organic eggs, too, are laid by hens that are able to range freely during the day. In addition, they are fed organically grown feed and can forage on pasture that is grown without chemicals.

Barn-laid eggs come from chickens that are kept in large sheds and they are free to roam within the shed. However, there is no standard maximum stocking density for the hens, so the amount of space they actually have for 'roaming' varies. Eggs labelled 'cage free' are essentially barn-laid eggs.

Cage eggs come from chickens that are housed in small cages, with three to five chickens per cage. These cages are stacked on top of each other in large sheds. A shed might contain up to 100,000 chickens. For obvious reasons, cage eggs draw the most criticism from animal welfare groups.

Nutritionally, there are no remarkable differences between the different eggs. However, true free-range hens – those that can forage for their food – tend to produce eggs with less cholesterol and higher levels of omega-3s and vitamins than cage or barn-laid eggs.

Many people (I'm one of them) argue that there is a huge difference in the taste of eggs produced by the various methods, mainly as a result of what the chickens eat. Diet can also influence the colour of the yolk. Many chickens (including those whose eggs are labelled free-range) are provided with feed that has pigments added to it to colour the yolks.

But, nutrition aside, the main motivation for buying free-range eggs comes down to people's perceptions of animal welfare and objections to cages and overcrowded barns where hens cannot exhibit their natural behavioural patterns. Be aware of the various standards used in defining free-range production, and look for standards that meet *your* ethical requirements. Even better, try to buy eggs from your local farmers' market, from a supplier you trust.

For more information on the terms 'free-range', 'organic' and 'certified organic', see pages 67–68.

TO SUM IT ALL UP

- Nuts and seeds are rich in protein and heart-healthy fats. Aim to eat one serve (30 g/1 oz) per day to reap the benefits.
- Eggs are also an excellent source of protein and are packed with nutrients. Two eggs constitute 1 serve of protein.
- There is negligible nutritional difference between raw and roasted nuts, but if you prefer them roasted, look for nuts with no added salt or flavourings.
- Nut and seed butters are nutritious spreads and it's easy to make your own. The healthiest versions contain no added salt or sugar.
- Eggs contain cholesterol, but this is not problematic for most people, unless they already have high blood cholesterol. Generally, it's saturated fats and trans fats that affect blood cholesterol, not the cholesterol content of foods.
- Omega-3 eggs contain less saturated fat and higher levels of omega-3s than conventional eggs. This is because the hens that lay them are fed a diet high in omega-3-rich seeds.
- Egg labels can be misleading. Read them carefully and look for standards that meet your requirements, whether that means organic, free-range, barn-laid or cage eggs.

QUINOA AND CRANBERRY PORRIDGE WITH POWER SEED SPRINKLE

(see recipe page 98)

NUTTY BUCKWHEAT GRANOLA
WITH DATES AND SEEDS
(see recipe page 99)

QUINOA AND CRANBERRY PORRIDGE
WITH POWER SEED SPRINKLE

Quinoa works beautifully in this warming porridge. Naturally gluten free, this grain is rich in plant protein and contains all the essential amino acids. The sweetened dried cranberries add a little natural tanginess and the sprinkling of seeds gives a good dose of essential fatty acids.

Preparation time: 10 minutes
Cooking time: 15 minutes
Serves 4

200 g (7 oz/1 cup) quinoa, rinsed

250 ml (9 fl oz/1 cup) milk, plus extra to serve (see tips)

40 g (1½ oz/¼ cup) sweetened dried cranberries

½ teaspoon natural vanilla extract

POWER SEED SPRINKLE

40 g (1½ oz/¼ cup) sunflower seeds

40 g (1½ oz/¼ cup) pepitas (pumpkin seeds)

1 tablespoon linseeds (flaxseeds)

1 tablespoon sesame seeds

1 teaspoon brown sugar

½ teaspoon ground cinnamon

For the power seed sprinkle, preheat the oven to 180°C (375°F). Line a large baking tray with baking paper. Combine all the ingredients and spread over the tray. Bake for 5 minutes or until lightly toasted. Cool.

Meanwhile, combine the quinoa and 500 ml (2 cups/17 fl oz) cold water in a large saucepan. Bring to the boil over medium heat, cover, reduce the heat to low and simmer for 10 minutes. Add the milk, cranberries and vanilla and cook, stirring, for 5 minutes or until the porridge is thick and creamy.

Serve the porridge topped with a little power seed sprinkle (you will have some left over for next time) and with milk.

+ TIPS +

For a dairy-free version, use soy, almond or rice milk.

The power seed sprinkle will keep in an airtight container for up to 2 weeks.

(pictured page 96)

NUTTY BUCKWHEAT GRANOLA
WITH DATES AND SEEDS

This is a baked granola recipe you can feel really good about! Unlike most commercial granolas, it contains no added oil and is sweetened only with the natural sugars from the date purée. Full of nuts and seeds, it's rich and filling, so you don't need a large serving. I like to sprinkle 2 tablespoons over natural yoghurt and fresh fruit.

Preparation time: 20 minutes
Cooking time: 35 minutes
Makes about 500 g (1 lb 2 oz/3 cups)

100 g (3^1/$_2$ oz) medjool dates,
pitted and chopped

2 teaspoons natural vanilla extract

1 teaspoon ground cinnamon

195 g (7 oz/1 cup) buckwheat kernels

40 g (1^1/$_2$ oz/^{1}/$_4$ cup) pepitas
(pumpkin seeds)

40 g (1^1/$_2$ oz/^{1}/$_4$ cup) sunflower seeds

40 g (1^1/$_2$ oz/^{1}/$_4$ cup) raw walnut halves,
roughly chopped

30 g (1 oz/^{1}/$_4$ cup) unsalted raw cashew
nuts, roughly chopped

35 g (1^1/$_4$ oz/^{1}/$_2$ cup) shredded coconut

20 g (^{3}/$_4$ oz/1 cup) puffed millet

Soak the dates in 80 ml (2^1/$_2$ fl oz/^{1}/$_3$ cup) of boiling water for 10 minutes. Transfer the dates and liquid to a food processor, add the vanilla and cinnamon and process to a smooth paste.

Preheat the oven to 150°C (300°F). Line a large baking tray with baking paper.

Combine the buckwheat, seeds and nuts in a bowl, add the date paste and toss until evenly coated. Spread in a single layer on the tray.

Bake for 30 minutes or until golden and crisp, stirring every 10 minutes. Add the coconut and millet and bake for 3–4 minutes or until the coconut is just golden. Cool completely before serving.

✦ TIPS ✦

The granola will keep in an airtight container for up to 4 weeks.

(pictured page 97)

KALE EGGS
WITH SMOKED SALMON AND BROCCOLINI

I love eggs for breakfast. Packed with protein, they really stay the course and keep me full until lunchtime. A serve of veggies at breakfast not only adds a good amount of dietary fibre, but is a great way to increase your overall intake for the day.

Preparation time: 10 minutes
Cooking time: 5 minutes
Serves 2

180 g (6$1/4$ oz) broccolini,
cut into short lengths

4 eggs

2 tablespoons milk (see tip)

1 teaspoon olive oil

1 garlic clove, crushed

50 g (1$3/4$ oz) kale, chopped

75 g (2$3/4$ oz) sliced smoked
salmon

Lime wedges, to serve

Steam the broccolini for 2 minutes, then drain.

Whisk the eggs and milk together. Season with sea salt and freshly ground black pepper.

Heat the oil in a frying pan over medium heat. Add the broccolini and garlic and cook, stirring, for 1 minute. Add the kale, stir until just wilted and remove from the pan.

Reduce the heat to low–medium. Add the egg and stir gently with a wooden spoon, bringing the egg from the edge of the pan to the centre. Continue until almost set. Gently stir in the broccolini mixture and season to taste.

Serve hot with smoked salmon and a squeeze of lime juice.

+ **TIP** +
For a dairy-free version, use soy, rice or almond milk.

SALAD OF SOFT-BOILED EGGS AND BABY GREENS
WITH BUTTERMILK DRESSING

Eggs are one of nature's superfoods. A source of complete protein, they're also an inexpensive non-meat source of vitamin B_{12}, which is found almost exclusively in animal products, making them perfect for vegetarians. In this light, delicious salad, buttermilk provides a low-fat creamy alternative to the usual mayonnaise-based dressings.

Preparation time: 20 minutes
Cooking time: 5 minutes
Serves 6 as a side dish or 4 as
 a light meal

6 eggs

1 bunch asparagus (about 8 spears),
cut into 4 cm (1^1/2 inch) lengths

150 g (5^1/2 oz) sugar snap peas,
halved diagonally

75 g (2^3/4 oz/1^1/2 cups) baby English
spinach leaves

2 baby cos (romaine) lettuces,
leaves separated

^{1}/2 firm avocado, sliced

2 tablespoons snipped chives

BUTTERMILK DRESSING

60 ml (2 fl oz/^{1}/4 cup) buttermilk

2 teaspoons chopped dill

2 teaspoons chopped flat-leaf
(Italian) parsley

2 teaspoons lemon juice

1 teaspoon dijon mustard

1 small French shallot, finely chopped

For the buttermilk dressing, put all the ingredients in a jar with a screw-top lid and shake well.

Place the eggs in a saucepan and cover with cold water. Bring to the boil, reduce the heat to low–medium and simmer for 4 minutes (see tip). Drain, refresh under cold water and carefully peel off the shells.

Meanwhile, steam the asparagus and sugar snap peas for 2 minutes or until just tender. Refresh under cold running water.

Arrange the spinach leaves, cos, asparagus and sugar snap peas on a plate. Cut the eggs in half and top the salad with the eggs and avocado. Drizzle with the buttermilk dressing and sprinkle with chives.

+ TIP +

If you prefer your eggs hard-boiled, cook them for 6–7 minutes.

Buttermilk dressing can be kept in the fridge for up to 1 week.

ROASTED NUT AND CACAO BUTTER

Making your own nut butter is really easy, and you can use any combination of nuts you like. If it's too thick, add a little macadamia oil to achieve the consistency you want.

Preparation time: 10 minutes
Cooking time: 10 minutes
Makes 480 g (1 lb 1 oz/3 cups)

155 g (5¹/2 oz/1 cup) unsalted raw cashew nuts

155 g (5¹/2 oz/1 cup) unsalted natural almonds

155 g (5¹/2 oz/1 cup) unsalted raw macadamia nuts

2 tablespoons raw cacao powder, sifted

1 teaspoon natural vanilla extract

Preheat the oven to 160°C (315°F). Line a large baking tray with baking paper. Spread the nuts in a single layer on the tray and roast for 10 minutes or until light golden. Set aside to cool (see tips).

Transfer the nuts to a high-powered blender or food processor. Blend on high speed for 6–8 minutes or until the nuts have formed a thick paste, scraping down the sides of the blender every 1–2 minutes. Add the cacao and vanilla and process until well combined.

✦ TIPS ✦

The time it takes for the nuts to form a paste will depend on the power of your blender. Processing them while they're still slightly warm helps them break down a little more quickly.

This nut butter will keep in an airtight jar in a cool dark place for up to 1 month.

CASHEW 'CHEESE'

Try this spread on crackers or used as a dip with vegetable sticks. It can even stand in for cheese sauce (see page 127).

Preparation time: 10 minutes, plus 3 hours soaking
Cooking time: None
Makes 400 g (14 oz/2 cups)

235 g (8¹/2 oz/1¹/2 cups) unsalted raw cashew nuts

1 tablespoon lemon juice

2 teaspoons white wine vinegar

2 teaspoons dijon mustard

125 ml (4 fl oz/¹/2 cup) coconut milk or water (see tips)

Place the cashews in a large bowl, cover with cold water and soak for 3 hours. Drain.

Combine the cashews, lemon juice, vinegar and mustard in a blender. Blend on high speed, gradually adding the coconut milk, until the cashews are smooth and have the consistency of thick cream cheese.

✦ TIPS ✦

Blending the nuts with coconut milk rather than water gives a creamier result.

This cashew 'cheese' will keep in an airtight container in the fridge for up to 3 days.

SWEET POTATO AND GOAT'S CHEESE FRITTATA
WITH LOTS OF GREENS

Eggs are a wonderful, inexpensive source of protein (6 g per egg) and by using them in a frittata you can combine them with lots of veggies – it's a great way to empty your crisper. What's more, you can enjoy this dish at any time of day.

Preparation time: 25 minutes
Cooking time: 1 hour 5 minutes
Serves 6

400 g (14 oz) orange sweet potato, cut into 1.5 cm (5/8 inch) dice

Olive oil spray

150 g (5 1/2 oz) green beans, cut into 1 cm (1/2 inch) lengths

150 g (5 1/2 oz) broccoli, cut into small florets

1 bunch asparagus (about 8 spears), cut into 1 cm (1/2 inch) lengths

8 eggs

2 tablespoons milk

1/4 cup chopped herbs, such as chives, parsley and mint

75 g (2 3/4 oz) goat's cheese, crumbled

Salad leaves, to serve

ROASTED CAPSICUM SALSA

2 tablespoons hazelnuts

120 g (4 1/4 oz) roasted red capsicum (pepper), chopped (see tips)

1 tablespoon snipped chives

1 teaspoon white balsamic vinegar

Preheat the oven to 200°C (400°F) and line a large baking tray with baking paper. Spread the sweet potato on the tray and spray lightly with olive oil. Roast for 25–30 minutes or until golden and tender.

Meanwhile, steam the beans, broccoli and asparagus until just tender. Refresh and drain well.

Whisk the eggs, milk, herbs and half the goat's cheese in a large bowl. Season with sea salt and freshly ground black pepper. Stir in the sweet potato and steamed vegetables.

Reduce the oven to 180°C (350°F). Line the base and sides of a 22 cm (8 1/2 inch) round tin with baking paper. Pour in the egg mixture, distributing the vegetables evenly. Dot the top with the remaining goat's cheese. Bake for 35 minutes or until puffed, golden and firm.

Meanwhile, for the roasted capsicum salsa, spread the hazelnuts on a tray and lightly toast in the oven for 10 minutes. Wrap them in a tea towel and rub off the skins. Cool, chop and mix with the capsicum, chives and vinegar.

Serve the frittata with the roasted capsicum salsa and salad leaves.

+ TIPS +

Roasted capsicum is available from delicatessens. Alternatively, you can roast your own: you will need 1 large capsicum for this recipe.

The frittata will keep, covered, in the fridge for up to 3 days. It can be eaten warm or cold, and leftovers are ideal for lunch boxes.

JAPANESE PANCAKES
WITH MUSHROOMS AND CHICKEN

Filled with shredded vegetables, minced lean chicken and protein-packed eggs, this version of a Japanese pancake makes a nutritious and filling lunch or light dinner. In Japan it's traditionally served with mayonnaise, but I prefer to skip this in favour of a little sweet soy sauce and some salad leaves.

Preparation time: 20 minutes
Cooking time: 35 minutes
Makes 8

75 g (2³/₄ oz/¹/₂ cup) wholemeal spelt flour or plain (all-purpose) flour

3 eggs

1¹/₂ tablespoons peanut or macadamia oil

200 g (7 oz) minced (ground) chicken or pork

150 g (5¹/₂ oz) mushrooms, finely chopped

2 teaspoons finely grated ginger

1 garlic clove, crushed

130 g (4¹/₂ oz/1³/₄ cups) shredded savoy cabbage

1 large carrot, coarsely grated

Sweet soy sauce, for drizzling

2 teaspoons sesame seeds, lightly toasted

Sliced spring onions (scallions), to serve

Baby kale leaves, to serve

Whisk together the flour, eggs and 80 ml (2¹/₂ fl oz/¹/₃ cup) cold water until smooth. Season with sea salt and freshly ground black pepper.

Heat 2 teaspoons of the oil in a large non-stick frying pan. Add the chicken and cook, breaking it up with a wooden spoon, for 5 minutes or until browned. Add the mushrooms, ginger and garlic and cook, stirring, for 3 minutes or until golden. Leave to cool completely.

Stir the chicken mixture, cabbage and carrot into the egg batter.

Heat half the remaining oil in a large non-stick frying pan over medium–high heat. Ladle ¹/₂ cup of batter per pancake into the pan and spread out to 1 cm (¹/₂ inch) thick. Cook for 3 minutes each side or until golden. Transfer to a plate and keep warm while you cook the rest, adding a little more oil when necessary.

Serve the pancakes drizzled with a little sweet soy sauce and scattered with the sesame seeds, spring onions and kale leaves.

SEED AND PARMESAN
CRACKERS
(see recipe page 110)

SEED AND NUT BARS

(see recipe page 111)

SEED AND PARMESAN CRACKERS

These crackers couldn't be easier to make: they're simply seeds, water and a little parmesan. You could serve them with cheese, but they're also delicious on their own. The linseeds are essential, because, when mixed with water, they form a gel that binds the ingredients and holds the crackers together. Apart from the linseeds, you can use pretty much any combination of seeds you like.

Preparation time: 10 minutes,
    plus 15 minutes soaking
Cooking time: 55 minutes
Makes 24

55 g (2 oz/$\frac{1}{3}$ cup) linseeds (flaxseeds)

55 g (2 oz/$\frac{1}{3}$ cup) pepitas (pumpkin seeds)

2 tablespoons sesame seeds

2 tablespoons chia seeds

1 tablespoon poppy seeds

25 g (1 oz/$\frac{1}{4}$ cup) finely grated parmesan cheese (see tips)

2 teaspoons chopped thyme

$\frac{1}{2}$ teaspoon sea salt

Combine the seeds in a bowl with 185 ml (6 fl oz/$\frac{3}{4}$ cup) water and leave to soak for 15 minutes. Stir in the parmesan, thyme and salt.

Meanwhile, preheat the oven to 150°C (300°F). Line a 25 x 38 cm (10 x 15 inch) baking tray with baking paper.

Wet your hands and press the seed mixture firmly onto the tray in a very thin, even layer. Press with the back of a spoon to smooth the surface. Lightly score into 24 squares.

Bake for 50–55 minutes or until golden and crisp (see tips). Cool completely on the tray, then break into crackers along score marks.

+ TIPS +

For a vegetarian version, use parmesan made with non-animal rennet.

These crackers will continue to harden as they cool. They can be stored in an airtight container for up to 1 week.

(pictured page 108)

SEED AND NUT BARS

Most commercially made nut bars contain a lot of sugar. Making your own means you know exactly what goes into them. Nuts are very satisfying, but also extremely energy dense, so portion size is the key.

Preparation time: 15 minutes
Cooking time: 20 minutes
Makes 20

280 g (10 oz/2 cups) unsalted raw nuts, such as almonds, macadamia nuts and walnuts

75 g (2³/4 oz/¹/2 cup) sunflower seeds

75 g (2³/4 oz/¹/2 cup) pepitas (pumpkin seeds)

2 tablespoons chia seeds

2 tablespoons sesame seeds

2 teaspoons ground cinnamon

175 g (6 oz/¹/2 cup) honey (see tips)

2 tablespoons macadamia oil

2 teaspoons natural vanilla extract

Preheat the oven to 150°C (300°F). Line a 23 x 33 cm (9 x 13 inch) baking tray with baking paper.

Roughly chop the nuts, sunflower seeds and pepitas together in a food processor. Transfer to a large bowl and stir in the chia, sesame seeds and cinnamon.

Stir the honey, oil and vanilla in a small saucepan over low heat until well combined. Pour over the dry ingredients and stir well.

Wet your hands and press the mixture firmly onto the tray. Press with the back of a spoon to smooth the surface. Bake for 20 minutes or until deep golden brown. Cool completely on the tray, then refrigerate until chilled. Cut into bars or squares.

+ TIP +

For a vegan version, replace the honey with rice malt syrup.

These will keep for up to 2 weeks in an airtight container in the fridge.

(pictured page 109)

HAZELNUT AND RASPBERRY CAKE

Life is definitely too short not to eat cake! The trick to good health is to eat something you really enjoy, eat only a small piece, and eat it occasionally, not every day. This cake is made from ground hazelnuts, buckwheat flour and macadamia oil, so it's brimming with healthy fatty acids and it's both gluten and dairy free. The earthy flavour of buckwheat flour works perfectly with the nuttiness of the hazelnuts and the sweetness of the raspberries. I like to serve this with a dollop of Greek yoghurt or thick coconut yoghurt.

Preparation time: 15 minutes
Cooking time: 45 minutes
Serves 12

45 g (1½ oz/⅓ cup) buckwheat flour

1 teaspoon baking powder

1 teaspoon ground cinnamon

¼ teaspoon ground nutmeg

4 eggs

140 g (5 oz/⅔ cup) caster (superfine) sugar

200 g (7 oz) hazelnut meal

80 ml (2½ fl oz/⅓ cup) macadamia oil

Finely grated zest of 1 lemon

120 g (4¼ oz/1 cup) raspberries, plus extra to serve

Chopped toasted hazelnuts, to serve

Greek-style or thick coconut yoghurt, to serve (see tips)

Preheat the oven to 170°C (325°F). Lightly grease and line a 22 cm (8½ inch) round spring-form cake tin with baking paper.

Sift together the flour, baking powder and spices.

Use an electric mixer to beat the eggs and sugar until pale and thick. Fold in the spiced flour mixture, hazelnut meal, oil, lemon zest and half the raspberries.

Spoon into the tin and decorate the top with the remaining raspberries. Bake for 40–45 minutes or until golden and a skewer poked into the centre comes out clean. If the cake browns too quickly, cover the top with foil. Cool in the tin for 10 minutes, then remove the sides of the tin and cool completely on a wire rack.

Scatter with hazelnuts and raspberries and serve with yoghurt.

+ TIPS +

For a dairy-free version, serve the cake with coconut yoghurt.

This will keep in an airtight container in a cool dark place for 4 days.

FROM THE VEGETABLE PATCH

FROM THE VEGETABLE PATCH

Vegetables are one of nature's best examples of a whole food: completely unrefined, unprocessed goodness. Vegetables are simply edible plants and you can eat many of their parts: seeds, leaves, tubers, stems, fruit, bulbs, even their flowers.

THEY'RE GOOD FOR US, AREN'T THEY?

Vegetables aren't just good for us: they contain nutrients that are essential for human life. They are versatile, can usually be eaten raw or cooked and, like all whole foods, are highly nutritious, being excellent sources of vitamins, fibre, folate and potassium as well as various minerals. Vegetables also provide small quantities of protein, sugars and starches. They are extremely low in kilojoules and fat, meaning that you can eat lots of them compared to many other foods, which is a good thing – especially if you're watching your weight.

HOW MANY SERVES SHOULD WE EAT?

Most of us don't eat nearly enough vegetables. On average we consume only half the minimum five serves per day recommended by most dietary guidelines.

Eating enough vegetables is essential for good health and weight management. Rather than viewing them as something we eat 'on the side', we should be thinking of vegetables as the 'main event', with other foods such as meat or grains being served on the side in smaller portions. If you imagine a dinner plate, always try to make sure that at least half the plate is vegetable based. Even if you're eating pasta this is possible. Make sure the portion of pasta is small, load the sauce with veggies and serve it with a side salad rather than bread.

AND WHAT IS A SERVE?

- 1/2 cup cooked or raw dense vegetables, such as carrots, beans or legumes
- 1 cup leafy vegetables, such as lettuce or spinach
- 1/2 cup fresh vegetable juice

SIMPLE COLOUR-CODING

Different families of vegetables contain different phytochemicals. These are the chemical compounds that occur naturally in plants and help protect our bodies against disease. Traditional vegetable groupings – leafy veggies, tubers, brassicas, root vegetables – provide one set of clues to nutritional content, but I find it much simpler to use colour coding. A vegetable's colour is a guide to the phytochemicals it contains. The plant pigments responsible for the various colours are powerful antioxidants and provide protection for our cells. Each colour offers something different – see the table opposite – so if you can eat a rainbow of veggies in each meal, or each day, you're doing well.

ALL-YEAR-ROUND GOODNESS?

Vegetables, like all plants, are governed by the seasons. Sadly, the idea of locally grown, seasonal produce is becoming something of the past, with supermarkets now stocking most fruit and vegetables all year round. They can do this by sourcing from areas with different climates, transporting produce long distances or importing from overseas. Imported vegetables are usually fumigated with methyl bromide to comply with quarantine regulations. Next time you're in the supermarket take a look at how many of the fruit and vegetables are labelled imported. You might be shocked at just how many 'food miles' the vegetable department is racking up.

Produce can also now be held in cold storage to be marketed at a different time of year, when it would previously have been 'out of season'. But, when a vegetable is in season and plentiful, it's cheaper to buy than imports and tastes much better, too.

COLOUR	VEGETABLES	NUTRIENTS	BENEFITS
Red	Red capsicum (pepper) Radish Tomato	Phytochemicals – lycopene, ellagic acid	Protection against prostate cancer and reduced risk of heart attack
		Flavonoids	Reduces inflammation; antioxidant properties
		Vitamin C	Promotes iron absorption, assists wound healing
		Folate	Required for red blood cells
Purple, blue	Beetroot (beet) Eggplant (aubergine) Red cabbage Purple sweet potato	Antioxidants – anthocyanins	Reduced risk of cancer; improved memory
		Flavonoids	Good for cardiovascular health
Orange, yellow	Carrot Pumpkin (squash) Corn Sweet potato	Carotenoids – beta-carotene	Growth and cell development; healthy skin, gums and bones
		Lutein	Eye health (prevents macular degeneration)
		Flavonoids	Antioxidant properties
		Vitamin C	Promotes iron absorption; assists wound healing
Green	Spinach Kale Silverbeet (chard) Broccoli Peas Beans	Isothiocyanates	Anti-cancer properties
		Folic acid	Prevents neural tube defects in pregnancy
		Vitamin K	Essential for blood clotting
		Potassium	Promotes healthy blood pressure; helps maintain fluid balance
White, brown	Potato Cauliflower Garlic Onion Celeriac Mushrooms	Allicin (garlic, ginger)	Assists in lowering cholesterol and blood pressure
		Potassium	Promotes healthy blood pressure; helps maintain fluid balance
		Vitamin C	Promotes iron absorption; assists wound healing

HOW FRESH IS 'FRESH'?

From a nutritional perspective, fresh vegetables are those eaten within seven days of being picked – not when they hit the supermarket shelves. As soon as they're harvested, fresh vegetables (and fruit) start to produce enzymes that cause loss of colour, flavour and nutrients; and their quality continues to deteriorate as the time from harvest to consumption increases. Actual changes in nutritional value depend on the particular nutrient, the vegetable, post-harvest handling, storage and cooking.

The best way to ensure optimum freshness and taste is to grow your own (in an ideal world!) or buy from a producer you trust, perhaps at a local farmers' market, where produce should be not only in season and picked at peak ripeness, but also grown locally. Supermarket produce is, at very best, three to seven days old before you even buy it.

FRESH VERSUS FROZEN

The mention of frozen vegetables might make you remember soggy, overcooked beans of your childhood. But frozen veggies don't have to be this way.

In fact, frozen produce is generally picked at peak ripeness and then blanched by being immersed briefly in boiling water or steamed to kill bacteria and stop the action of enzymes that would otherwise cause it to lose colour, flavour and nutrients. After blanching, it is snap-frozen. Snap freezing locks the veggies in a relatively nutrient-rich state and they will last for months in an airtight bag if kept at around -18°C (-0.4°F). Vegetables with a high water content, such as Asian greens, don't freeze well, but denser vegetables such as peas and corn freeze very successfully.

Without a doubt, you can't beat fresh, seasonal veggies for optimal flavour and texture, and they are definitely my preference, but frozen vegetables have their place. It might surprise you to find out that nutritionally, frozen veggies often come out in front of 'not so fresh' fresh produce, due to the rapid deterioration of nutrients in fresh produce.

Frozen vegetables are ideal when vegetables are out of season, especially those with a short season such as broad beans or peas. Also, the price is fixed and doesn't fluctuate throughout the year. A trick to keeping frozen veggies more delicious is not to ever let them thaw before cooking or they tend to become soggy. Cook them straight from the freezer and keep cooking to an absolute minimum.

In fact, cooking technique is possibly even more important, nutritionally speaking, than whether a vegetable is fresh or frozen. Cooking methods that use a minimum of water and are brief, such as steaming, stir-frying and even microwaving, are best. They minimise the loss of vitamins such as B_1, B_6, B_{12} and C, which are sensitive to both heat and light and start to deteriorate once cooked.

AND WHAT ABOUT CANNED?

Some canned vegetables have their uses – canned tomatoes and canned legumes are pantry staples in my house, being easy to prepare and nutritious.

The canning process involves cooking the vegetables, which can lead to the loss of heat-sensitive nutrients such as the B and C vitamins. In many cases it also involves adding salt, sugar, preservatives or firming agents to enhance flavour or extend shelf life. Additives vary enormously across different vegetables and different brands. Some brands of tinned tomatoes, for example, contain 10 times as much added salt as others. Check the labels for additives and look for products that contain little or no added salt or sugar. Keep any eye out for other additives that might sneak in, too.

IS RAW ALWAYS BEST?

Raw diets seem to be getting a lot of attention lately, but are they actually healthier?

When it comes to vegetables, many – such as kale and broccoli – are most nutritious in their raw state. But there are others – particularly tomatoes, carrots and asparagus – that require heat to release some nutrients. And many of the vegetables we are used to eating cooked are also delicious raw: try shredding some raw silverbeet (Swiss chard), Brussels sprouts or bok choy (pak choy) into your next salad.

VEGETABLE JUICES

When it comes to juices, there's no argument: fresh is definitely best. Bottled veggie juices often contain added salt or sugar, or in fact contain more fruit juice than vegetable juice. Shelf-stable vegetable juices, the ones you find in the drinks aisle and not in the refrigerated section, have undergone heat treatment, which kills bacteria but also destroys antioxidants.

Juices are a big 'health' market at the moment, but you need to read the label carefully to check whether what you're looking at is genuinely a healthy choice.

Freshly pressed vegetable juices, or fruit and veggie combos, on the other hand, are a great way to add a couple of extra serves to your daily intake.

However, on the downside, most domestic juicers extract the juice and leave behind the pulp... and with that pulp goes most of the vegetable's dietary fibre. You do, however, gain all the vitamins, minerals and antioxidant phytochemicals, which is a big win. Some new juicers work more like blenders and retain all the pulp, so you gain the benefits of the fibre as well.

HOW CAN I REACH THAT MAGICAL FIVE SERVES A DAY?

Veggies at breakfast Try adding a large handful of spinach or kale to your breakfast smoothie – you won't even taste it. Add some spinach, vine-ripened tomatoes or mushrooms to your poached or scrambled eggs.

Lunchtime Instead of a sandwich, try a chopped vegetable salad. Include some legumes or lean meat for protein to help fill you up. If you do opt for a sandwich, make sure it has at least three salad fillings.

Get juicing Replace half the fruit in your fresh juice with vegetables. Carrots, beetroot, kale and celery are all perfect additions.

Snacks Add veggies at snack time, such as vegetable sticks with home-made hummus, lettuce wraps filled with grated veggies and tzatziki, or roasted chickpeas.

Dinnertime Make sure at least half your plate is vegetable based. It's super-easy to do with stir-fries or warm salads, but even if you're having a curry, pasta or risotto you can still load it up with veggies.

Meat-free Mondays Nominate one night a week to be vegetarian for dinner. Not only will it make you try new things, your body will thank you for it.

TO SUM IT ALL UP

- Vegetables are nutritious whole foods packed with vitamins, fibre, folate, potassium and minerals. Aim to eat at least 5 serves per day.
- Include a variety of different coloured vegetables in your diet. Colour is a guide to phytochemical content and each colour has unique properties when it comes to protecting against disease.
- Vegetables in season are more plentiful, fresher and cheaper than imported or cold-stored out-of-season ones.
- Frozen vegetables are snap-frozen and can be a good option for produce that has a short season or is expensive.
- Canned vegetables can be handy pantry staples. Look for brands with minimal or no added salt or sugar.
- Include a mix of both raw and cooked vegetables in your diet.
- Fresh juices can be a good way to increase your daily serves of vegetables. But be aware that most juicers leave the pulp behind, including most of the dietary fibre.

WHOLEGRAIN SPELT SPAGHETTI
WITH ZUCCHINI, ALMONDS, BEANS AND TOMATOES

When it comes to pasta, I always choose a wholegrain variety. Spelt is not only higher in protein and dietary fibre than regular wheat pasta, it's also gentler on the digestion. Packing the sauce with lots of vegetables will help you keep the portion of pasta to a sensible size.

Preparation time: 15 minutes
Cooking time: 15 minutes
Serves 4

400 g (14 oz) grape tomatoes

Olive oil spray

250 g (9 oz) wholegrain spelt spaghetti

150 g (5¹/2 oz) green beans, sliced

1 tablespoon olive oil

2 garlic cloves, crushed

2 teaspoons finely grated lemon zest

2 large zucchini (courgettes), grated

35 g (1¹/4 oz/¹/3 cup) flaked almonds, toasted

2 tablespoons chopped flat-leaf (Italian) parsley

2 tablespoons chopped mint

1 tablespoon lemon juice

80 g (2³/4 oz/¹/3 cup) ricotta cheese

Preheat the oven to 180°C (350°F). Line a large baking tray with baking paper. Place the tomatoes on the tray and spray lightly with olive oil. Roast for 8–10 minutes or until the tomatoes are just wilted.

Meanwhile, cook the pasta in lightly salted boiling water until al dente. Add the beans for the last 2 minutes of the cooking time. Drain and return the pasta and beans to the saucepan.

Heat the olive oil in a large non-stick frying pan over medium heat. Cook the garlic and lemon zest, stirring, for 30 seconds or until fragrant. Add the zucchini and cook, stirring, for 1–2 minutes or until bright green. Be careful not to overcook the zucchini.

Add the zucchini mixture, half the almonds, the roasted tomatoes, parsley, mint and lemon juice to the pasta and toss gently. Season to taste with sea salt and freshly ground black pepper. Serve topped with the remaining almonds and a dollop of ricotta.

SPROUT, MINT AND PANCETTA
SALAD WITH PECORINO
(see recipe page 124)

KALE, QUINOA AND MINT TABBOULI
(see recipe page 125)

SPROUT, MINT AND PANCETTA SALAD
WITH PECORINO

Eating more raw vegetables is something we can all benefit from. Brussels sprouts and silverbeet are usually served cooked, but in this salad they're simply shredded and eaten as a delicious salad green. Both are packed with flavonoids (compounds that may offer protection against some cancers) as well as being rich in vitamin C and fibre.

Preparation time: 15 minutes
Cooking time: 10 minutes
Serves 4 as a side dish

2 tablespoons pine nuts

75 g (2³/4 oz) pancetta, diced
(optional; see tips)

350 g (12 oz) brussels sprouts,
shredded

150 g (5¹/2 oz) silverbeet (Swiss chard),
centre vein removed, shredded
(see tips)

¹/4 cup mint, shredded

¹/4 cup flat-leaf (Italian) parsley,
chopped

25 g (1 oz/¹/4 cup) finely grated
pecorino cheese, plus extra to serve

1 tablespoon extra virgin olive oil

1 tablespoon lemon juice

1 teaspoon dijon mustard (see tips)

1 French shallot, finely chopped

Heat a small non-stick frying pan over medium heat. Add the pine nuts and cook, stirring, for 2 minutes or until lightly toasted. Remove from the pan and set aside to cool.

Add the pancetta to the pan and cook, stirring, for 3–4 minutes or until golden. Remove and set aside to cool.

Combine the toasted pine nuts, pancetta, brussels sprouts, silverbeet, mint, parsley and pecorino in a large bowl.

Whisk together the oil, lemon juice, mustard and shallot. Add the dressing to the salad, toss gently and serve with extra pecorino.

✦ TIPS ✦

For a gluten-free version, use gluten-free pancetta and mustard.

You can replace the silverbeet with 150 g (5¹/2 oz) shredded curly kale.

(pictured page 122)

KALE, QUINOA AND MINT TABBOULI

Quinoa and kale give this version of tabbouli a gluten-free modern twist. Kale is loaded with vitamin C, which assists immunity; beta-carotene, which is essential for eye health; and antioxidants, which help protect against cancer. Dates add natural sweetness and toasted pepitas a delicious crunch.

Preparation time: 20 minutes
Cooking time: 15 minutes
Serves 4

95 g (3¼ oz/½ cup) quinoa, rinsed and drained

300 g (10½ oz/about ½ bunch) kale, centre vein removed

Olive oil spray

200 g (7 oz) grape tomatoes, chopped

2 Lebanese (short) cucumbers, seeded and diced

¼ cup mint leaves, chopped

¼ cup flat-leaf (Italian) parsley, chopped

2 tablespoons pepitas (pumpkin seeds), lightly toasted

40 g (1½ oz) pitted dates, finely chopped

1 tablespoon lemon juice

1 tablespoon extra virgin olive oil

Put the quinoa and 250 ml (9 fl oz/1 cup) cold water in a saucepan over medium heat. Bring to the boil, cover, reduce the heat to low and simmer for 12 minutes or until the water has evaporated and the quinoa is al dente. Set aside to cool completely.

Meanwhile, preheat the oven to 200°C (400°F) and line a baking tray with baking paper. Tear the kale into bite-sized pieces, place in a single layer on the tray and spray with olive oil. Bake for 8–10 minutes until crisp and golden. Season to taste with sea salt and leave to cool completely.

Toss half the kale with the quinoa, tomatoes, cucumber, mint, parsley, pepitas and dates in a large bowl. Whisk together the lemon juice and olive oil, add the dressing to the salad and toss well. Season to taste and serve topped with the remaining crisp kale.

(pictured page 123)

ROASTED VEGETABLE STACK
WITH CASHEW 'CHEESE'

Even the most committed meat-eater will love this vegetable stack. The lentils in the tomato sauce add protein, the mushrooms are rich in B vitamins and the cashew 'cheese' is a delicious stand-in for the traditional cheese sauce. What's more, the cashews offer a good dose of healthy fats and magnesium, assisting heart health.

Preparation time: 30 minutes
Cooking time: 1 hour
Serves 6

850 g (1 lb 14 oz) sweet potato, cut into thin rounds

1 large eggplant (aubergine) (about 550 g/1 lb 4 oz), cut into 5 mm (1/4 inch) slices

Olive oil spray

1 tablespoon olive oil, plus 1 teaspoon extra for drizzling

1 red onion, finely chopped

200 g (7 oz) mushrooms, sliced

2 garlic cloves, crushed

2 x 400 g (14 oz) tins diced tomatoes

70 g (2 1/2 oz/1/3 cup) red lentils, rinsed

1/4 cup basil leaves, plus extra to garnish

3 large zucchini (courgettes)

1 quantity cashew 'cheese' (see page 102)

Preheat the oven to 200°C (400°F) and line 2 large trays with baking paper. Place the sweet potato and the eggplant on the trays and spray them with olive oil. Roast for 30 minutes, turning and swapping the trays halfway through cooking, until golden and tender.

Meanwhile, heat the olive oil in a large saucepan over medium heat. Cook the onion, stirring, for 5 minutes or until softened. Add the mushrooms and cook, stirring, for 3–4 minutes or until browned. Add the garlic and stir for 30 seconds. Add the tomatoes, lentils and 170 ml (5 1/2 fl oz/2/3 cup) water and bring to the boil. Reduce the heat to low and simmer, partially covered, for 25 minutes or until the lentils are tender and the sauce is thick. Stir in the basil and season to taste.

Cut the zucchini into long ribbons with a vegetable peeler, stopping when you reach the seeds.

Lightly spray a 2 litre (70 fl oz/8 cup) ovenproof dish with olive oil. Spread 1/2 cup of the tomato mixture in the dish. Arrange a third of the zucchini ribbons overlapping in a single layer on top of the tomato.

Top with half the eggplant and half the sweet potato. Spread with half the cashew cheese and half the remaining tomato mixture.

Repeat with half the remaining zucchini and all the remaining eggplant, sweet potato, cashew cheese and tomato mixture.

Finish with a layer of zucchini and drizzle with the extra oil. Bake for 20–25 minutes or until bubbling. Leave for 5 minutes before cutting, and serve garnished with basil.

ROASTED BROCCOLI AND CHICKPEA SALAD
WITH HERBED TAHINI DRESSING

Broccoli is a true superfood, packed with disease- and cancer-fighting compounds and rich in vitamin C, beta-carotene, folate, iron and potassium. Nutty chickpeas are not only low GI, they're packed with protein and dietary fibre, making this salad filling and substantial enough for a light lunch or dinner.

Preparation time: 15 minutes
Cooking time: 20 minutes
Serves 4

1/2 cauliflower, cut into florets

Olive oil spray

300 g (10 1/2 oz) broccoli, cut into florets

1/4 cup chopped flat-leaf (Italian) parsley

2 tablespoons lemon juice

2 teaspoons olive oil

1 teaspoon garam masala

255 g (9 oz/1 1/2 cups) drained cooked chickpeas (see tips)

4 spring onions (scallions), thinly sliced

1 tablespoon unhulled tahini (see tips)

1 teaspoon honey (see tips)

1 1/2 tablespoons pine nuts, lightly toasted

Preheat the oven to 180°C (350°F). Line a large baking tray with baking paper. Place the cauliflower on the tray, spray lightly with olive oil and roast for 10 minutes. Add the broccoli, spray lightly and roast for a further 10 minutes or until golden and tender.

Meanwhile, combine 2 tablespoons of the parsley, 1 tablespoon of the lemon juice, the olive oil and the garam masala in a large bowl. Stir in the chickpeas and spring onions and leave for 5 minutes.

Combine the tahini, remaining parsley, remaining lemon juice, honey and 1–2 tablespoons warm water to make a thin dressing.

Stir the broccoli and cauliflower into the chickpea mixture. Pile the salad onto a plate, drizzle with dressing and sprinkle with pine nuts.

+ TIPS +

For a vegan version, replace the honey with maple syrup.

You can replace the chickpeas with a 400 g (14 oz) can of chickpeas.

Unhulled tahini is made from whole sesame seeds and is more nutritious than hulled tahini. Look for it in the health-food section of your supermarket.

PICK-ME-UP BEETROOT SOUP
WITH SPICED YOGHURT

CELERIAC AND LEEK SOUP WITH
HAZELNUTS AND CRISP SAGE

(see recipe page 132)

PICK-ME-UP BEETROOT SOUP
WITH SPICED YOGHURT

Beetroot are not only a good source of fibre, folate, manganese and potassium, they have also been used medicinally for centuries to help detoxify the liver. This soup, which combines beetroot with the natural aniseed flavour of fennel, is the perfect pick-me-up for when you're feeling sluggish. Beetroot's vibrant red-purple colour comes from betacyanins, plant pigments that act as powerful antioxidants.

Preparation time: 20 minutes
Cooking time: 1 hour 30 minutes
Serves 4

1 kg (2 lb 4 oz/about 5 large) beetroot (beets), scrubbed

1 tablespoon olive oil

1 leek, thinly sliced

1 small fennel bulb, chopped

3 celery stalks, diced

2 garlic cloves, crushed

1 teaspoon fennel seeds, crushed

750 ml (26 fl oz/3 cups) home-made or low-salt vegetable stock (see tips)

130 g (4$\frac{1}{2}$ oz/$\frac{1}{2}$ cup) natural yoghurt

$\frac{1}{2}$ teaspoon ground cumin

$\frac{1}{2}$ teaspoon ground coriander

Mint leaves, to garnish

Preheat the oven to 200°C (400°F). Place the beetroot in a large roasting tin and cover with foil. Roast for 1 hour or until tender when pierced with a skewer. Cool slightly, then peel and chop.

Heat the oil in a large saucepan over medium heat. Add the leek, chopped fennel and celery and cook, stirring, for 6–7 minutes or until softened. Add the garlic and fennel seeds and stir for 1 minute or until fragrant.

Add the stock and beetroot and bring to the boil. Reduce the heat and simmer, partially covered, for 20 minutes. Cool slightly, then blend the soup in batches. Return to the pan and heat through gently.

Stir together the yoghurt, cumin and coriander. Serve the soup topped with a dollop of spiced yoghurt and a sprinkle of mint.

✦ TIPS ✦

For a gluten-free version, use gluten-free stock.

This soup can be frozen in airtight containers for up to 2 months.

CELERIAC AND LEEK SOUP
WITH HAZELNUTS AND CRISP SAGE

Celeriac might be ugly on the outside, but beneath its lumpy surface the creamy white flesh of this large winter root vegetable has a unique mild celery flavour. Combined with leek and potato, it makes a deliciously smooth soup, perfect for a cold night.

Preparation time: 20 minutes
Cooking time: 30 minutes
Serves 4

40 g (1½ oz/¼ cup) hazelnuts

1½ tablespoons olive oil

1 leek, white part only, thinly sliced

2 garlic cloves, crushed

1 litre (35 fl oz/4 cups) home-made or low-salt vegetable or chicken stock (see tips)

1 celeriac (about 650 g/1 lb 7 oz), chopped

500 g (1 lb 2 oz) floury potatoes, such as russet burbank or sebago, chopped

24 small sage leaves

Preheat the oven to 180°C (350°F). Spread the hazelnuts on a baking tray and lightly toast for 10 minutes. Wrap the nuts in a tea towel and rub off the skins. Cool, then chop coarsely.

Heat 1 tablespoon of the oil in a large saucepan over medium–low heat. Cook the leek, stirring, for 6–7 minutes or until softened. Add the garlic and cook, stirring, for 1 minute or until aromatic.

Add the stock, celeriac and potato and bring to the boil. Reduce the heat to low and simmer, partially covered, for 20 minutes or until the celeriac and potato are very tender. Leave to cool slightly.

Blend the soup in batches until smooth. Return to the pan and heat through gently. Season to taste with sea salt and black pepper.

Meanwhile, heat the remaining oil in a small frying pan over medium heat and fry the sage leaves, stirring, for 1–2 minutes or until crisp. Drain on paper towel.

Serve the soup with the toasted hazelnuts and crisp sage leaves.

✦ TIPS ✦

For a gluten-free version, use gluten-free stock.

This soup can be frozen in airtight containers for up to 2 months.

(pictured page 130)

ROASTED CARROTS AND ASPARAGUS
WITH LEMON, HONEY AND THYME DRESSING

Purple carrots might seem exotic, but in fact they're thought to predate the regular orange variety. They gain their colour from anthocyanin, rather than the usual orange beta-carotene pigments; both pigments act as powerful antioxidants in the body. All carrots are rich in fibre, low in kilojoules and naturally sweet.

Preparation time: 10 minutes
Cooking time: 30 minutes
Serves 4 as a side dish

500 g (1 lb 2 oz) baby carrots, scrubbed and halved lengthways (see tips)

1 tablespoon olive oil

1 tablespoon honey (see tips)

2 teaspoons lemon juice

1 garlic clove, crushed

2 teaspoons chopped thyme leaves

2 bunches asparagus (about 16 spears)

Preheat the oven to 200°C (400°F). Line a large tray with baking paper. Toss the carrots with the olive oil, season with sea salt and freshly ground black pepper and arrange on the tray. Roast for 20 minutes.

Mix together the honey, lemon juice, garlic and thyme.

Add the asparagus to the carrots. Drizzle with the dressing and toss to coat well. Roast for 10 minutes or until golden and tender. Serve hot or at room temperature.

+ TIPS +

A combination of yellow, orange and purple carrots makes an especially colourful dish.

For a vegan version, replace the honey with maple syrup.

(pictured page 134)

ROASTED CARROTS AND
ASPARAGUS WITH LEMON,
HONEY AND THYME DRESSING

(see recipe page 133)

BARBECUED CORN WITH LIME AND SMOKED PAPRIKA

(see recipe page 136)

STIR-FRIED BROCCOLINI AND GREEN BEANS WITH SPICY SEEDS

(see recipe page 137)

BARBECUED CORN
WITH LIME AND SMOKED PAPRIKA

When it comes to barbecuing, nothing beats sweet corn, especially when it's teamed with lime and smoky paprika. Antioxidant carotenoids, lutein and zeaxanthin all promote healthy eye sight, and corn is packed with them. It's also rich in dietary fibre, which promotes a healthy bowel.

Preparation time: 10 minutes
Cooking time: 10 minutes
Serves 4 as a side dish

Olive oil spray

1 teaspoon smoked paprika

1 teaspoon finely grated lime zest

¼ teaspoon chilli flakes

3 tablespoons finely grated pecorino cheese (see tip)

1 tablespoon unsalted butter, melted

4 cobs corn, husks and silks removed

Lime wedges, to serve

Preheat a barbecue or chargrill pan to medium heat. Cut four 30 cm (12 inch) squares of foil and spray each piece with olive oil.

Mix together the paprika, lime zest, chilli and 2 tablespoons of the pecorino. Put each corn cob on a square of foil. Brush the corn cobs with melted butter, then sprinkle with the paprika mixture. Season each cob with sea salt and black pepper and wrap up in foil.

Barbecue the corn parcels, turning occasionally, for 8–10 minutes or until the corn is lightly charred and tender. Serve sprinkled with the remaining pecorino, with lime wedges to the side.

+ **TIP** +

For a vegetarian version, use pecorino (or parmesan) made with non-animal rennet.

(pictured page 135)

STIR-FRIED BROCCOLINI AND GREEN BEANS
WITH SPICY SEEDS

Stir-frying is a very quick way to cook vegetables, which means it minimises nutrient loss. Macadamia oil is perfect for stir-fries because it has a high smoke point (the temperature at which a cooking oil begins to break down); its delicious nutty taste is a bonus. It's also extremely rich in healthy monounsaturated fats.

Preparation time: 10 minutes
Cooking time: 10 minutes
Serves 4 as a side dish

1 tablespoon macadamia or peanut oil

360 g (12¾ oz) broccolini

200 g (7 oz) green beans

1 tablespoon pepitas (pumpkin seeds)

1 tablespoon sunflower seeds

4 garlic cloves, thinly sliced

1 teaspoon finely grated lemon zest

¼ teaspoon chilli flakes

Heat half the oil in a wok or large frying pan over high heat and stir-fry the broccolini and beans for 3–4 minutes or until just tender. Remove from the wok.

Reduce the heat to medium. Add the remaining oil and seeds and stir-fry for 2 minutes or until golden. Add the garlic, lemon zest and chilli and stir-fry for 30 seconds or until aromatic.

Return the broccolini and beans to the wok and stir-fry for 1 minute to heat through. Serve immediately.

(pictured page 135)

BAKED SWEET POTATOES
STUFFED WITH SPINACH, FETA AND PEPITAS

Like all orange and yellow vegetables, sweet potatoes are an excellent source of the powerful antioxidant beta-carotene, which has been linked to a reduced risk of cancer and heart disease. Roasting sweet potato concentrates its natural sweetness, and the slightly salty feta is a delicious contrast.

Preparation time: 15 minutes
Cooking time: 50 minutes
Serves 4

4 small sweet potatoes
(about 200 g/7 oz each), scrubbed

1 tablespoon olive oil

2 large red onions, thinly sliced

2 garlic cloves, thinly sliced

100 g (3^{1}/$_{2}$ oz/2^{1}/$_{4}$ cups) baby English spinach leaves

50 g (1^{3}/$_{4}$ oz) feta cheese, crumbled

2 tablespoons seedless raisins

1 tablespoon pepitas (pumpkin seeds), lightly toasted

1 tablespoon sunflower seeds, lightly toasted

Preheat the oven to 200°C (400°F). Prick the sweet potatoes well and roast for 40–50 minutes, turning once, until tender when pierced with a skewer.

Meanwhile, heat the olive oil in a large non-stick frying pan over low heat and cook the onion, stirring occasionally, for 8–10 minutes or until softened and light golden. Add the garlic and cook, stirring, for 1 minute. Add the spinach and stir until just wilted. Remove from the heat, add the feta, raisins and seeds and season to taste with sea salt and freshly ground black pepper.

Cut a slit in each baked potato. Mash the flesh lightly with a fork and spoon the filling into the potatoes.

RAINBOW SLAW

Different coloured vegetables all provide something unique nutritionally, so aim to eat a serving from each colour group every day. This multi-hued salad is brimming with disease-fighting phytonutrients.

Preparation time: 15 minutes
Cooking time: None
Serves 4–6

1/2 small red cabbage, shredded

2 carrots, cut into thin matchsticks

100 g (31/2 oz) sugar snap peas, thinly sliced

100 g (31/2 oz) snow peas (mangetout), thinly sliced

1 red capsicum (pepper), thinly sliced

2 tablespoons chopped mint

2 tablespoons chopped flat-leaf (Italian) parsley

2 tablespoons sultanas, coarsely chopped

1 tablespoon lemon juice

1 tablespoon olive oil

2 tablespoons unsalted roasted cashews, chopped

Combine the vegetables, herbs and sultanas in a large bowl.

Whisk together the lemon juice and olive oil, add the dressing to the salad and toss gently. Serve garnished with cashews.

ASPARAGUS AND SUGAR SNAP PEA SALAD
WITH PECANS AND DRIED CHERRIES

Delicate vegetables, such as asparagus and sugar snap peas, are best cooked by lightly steaming, because this method preserves the most nutrients. I like to toss the fennel in lemon with a touch of salt and sugar to lightly pickle it and bring out its natural sweetness.

Preparation time: 10 minutes
Cooking time: 2 minutes
Serves 4

2 bunches asparagus
(about 16 spears), halved

200 g (7 oz) sugar snap peas

1 fennel bulb, thinly sliced

1 tablespoon lemon juice

1 tablespoon olive oil

1/2 teaspoon caster (superfine) sugar

75 g (2³/4 oz/1²/3 cups) baby English spinach or rocket (arugula) leaves

40 g (1¹/2 oz/1/4 cup) dried cherries (see tip)

25 g (1 oz/1/4 cup) pecans, chopped

50 g (1³/4 oz) drained marinated feta cheese, crumbled

Place the asparagus and sugar snap peas in a steamer over a saucepan of simmering water. Cover and steam for 1–2 minutes or until tender-crisp. Refresh under cold running water. Drain well.

Mix together the fennel, half the lemon juice, half the olive oil, the sugar and a pinch of salt and set aside for 5 minutes.

Toss together the steamed vegetables, fennel, spinach, cherries and pecans in a large bowl. Drizzle with the remaining olive oil and lemon juice and serve topped with marinated feta.

+ TIP +

If you can't find dried cherries, sweetened dried cranberries work just as well.

FROM
THE SEA

FROM THE SEA

Fresh seafood is not only delicious to eat, but it's an extremely valuable and nutritious food source throughout the world. The seafood family is large and encompasses any form of sea life regarded as food by humans. Its main members are fish, shellfish (oysters, mussels and scallops, for example), crustaceans (prawns, shrimp, lobsters, crabs), cephalopods (octopus) and echinoderms (sea urchins, sea cucumbers).

WHAT MAKES SEAFOOD SO FAMOUSLY GOOD FOR US?

Most of us know that seafood is meant to be good for us, but what exactly makes it so nutritious? Well, it's packed with protein; in fact, it contains all nine of the essential amino acids, making it a source of complete protein. Even better, most seafood is considered to be low in kilojoules compared with many other protein-rich foods, such as red meat or chicken, which means you consume fewer kilojoules for the same amount of protein.

In addition to its impressively high protein content seafood is also rich in many other micronutrients. These include:

- zinc, for a healthy immune system, healthy growth and metabolic processes
- iron, to produce haemoglobin
- magnesium, for healthy bones, muscle function and energy metabolism
- iodine, essential for thyroid function
- selenium, an antioxidant that protects cell membranes
- vitamin B_{12}, essential for red blood cells and DNA
- vitamin A, important for healthy vision, skin and bones
- vitamin D, for calcium absorption, strong bones and strong teeth

And if that weren't enough, leaving the best until last, fish is a wonderful source of readily available healthy polyunsaturated fats, which are linked to a whole host of health benefits.

FABULOUS OMEGA-3 FATTY ACIDS

The long-chain unsaturated fatty acids found in fish are known as omega-3 fatty acids and they have been found to have a very important role in nutrition. Consuming less saturated fat and more omega-3s can help lower the blood's levels of cholesterol and triglycerides: two fats that, in excess, have been shown to increase the risk of heart disease.

Adequate intake of omega-3s can therefore reduce the risk of blood clotting and stroke and lower blood pressure. It can also reduce inflammation in the body and assist conditions such as rheumatoid arthritis and osteoarthritis. It's even linked to improved memory and assisting depression.

HOW MUCH SHOULD WE EAT?

Most dietary standards around the world recommend that to reduce the risk of heart disease we should eat at least two serves of fish per week, with one of those serves being 'oily' fish. The oiliest fish are the best sources of omega-3s. The Australian Heart Foundation takes it a step further and recommends we should be eating two or three serves of oily fish per week. Oily fish tend to be darker fleshed and stronger flavoured than 'white' fish and include small varieties such as kippers, sardines and anchovies, plus the larger tuna, salmon, mackerel, mullet and trevally.

AND WHAT IS A SERVE?

A standard serve is 100 g (3½ oz) cooked fish or one small can of fish such as salmon or tuna.

Dietary guidelines worldwide vary in their recommendations on omega-3 intake. For example, the Australian Heart Foundation recommends that people take in 500 mg omega-3s per day for general good health. The American Heart Association recommends that people with coronary heart disease take in 1 g of omega-3s per day.

To take in 500 mg of omega-3s from seafood, you would need to eat one serve of the following:

- 40 g (1¹/₂ oz) swordfish
- 60 g (2¹/₄ oz) Atlantic salmon
- 125 g (4¹/₂ oz) Spanish mackerel
- 150 g (5¹/₂ oz) mussels
- 165 g (5³/₄ oz) oysters
- 230 g (8 oz) snapper
- 280 g (10 oz) tiger prawns (shrimp)

AND WHAT ABOUT OMEGA-6?

Omega-6 is another type of polyunsaturated essential fatty acid. It is found mainly in seeds, nuts and vegetable oils, but fish also contains a small amount.

Omega-3s tend to have an anti-inflammatory effect in the body, whereas omega-6s have an inflammatory effect. For this reason it is important to eat a healthy ratio of omega-3s and omega-6s. The ratio in fish is excellent – it contains more than five times as much omega-6 as omega-3. This is a good thing because most people eat more omega-6 than omega-3.

FARMED OR WILD-CAUGHT?

You've probably noticed fish labelled 'farmed' or 'wild-caught' on restaurant menus or at your local fish shop. What do these terms really mean?

Fish caught directly from the sea, lakes or rivers, by line or net, is considered wild-caught. In contrast, fish cultivated in tanks, ponds or sea cages is regarded as 'farmed'.

Nutritionally, there are some differences between the two. Wild-caught fish has a similar protein content to farmed, but contains fewer calories. When it comes to fat content, farmed fish is in the lead, especially farmed salmon, which contains more omega-3 and omega-6 fatty acids. Farmed fish can also be higher in vitamins A and C, if these are added to their feed.

So which is better for us? Wild-caught fish sounds like the most natural option, right? The reality is that our current consumption of wild-caught fish is not sustainable. Natural fish stocks throughout the world are declining and farmed fish has emerged out of necessity. As a sustainably produced food, farmed fish has a valuable and essential place in our diet.

However, fish farming (aquaculture) brings its own challenges, such as the need for sustainable environmental practices and strict regulations to ensure correct and hygienic farming. These regulations vary widely across the globe. This means imported farmed fish and locally farmed fish are produced under different rules.

FRESH OR FROZEN?

Seafood is a highly perishable product, prone to spoiling if not consumed quickly or kept at a constant regulated temperature. For this reason, snap-freezing of seafood soon after harvesting is common. Nutritionally speaking, there is no significant difference between fresh and frozen fish, although during lengthy storage the omega-3 content will start to degrade. Depending on where you live, fresh fish can be difficult to source or expensive. In these circumstances frozen fish can be a good option.

Most seafood outlets sell a combination of fresh seafood and frozen-then-thawed seafood. Supermarkets also sell packaged frozen fish, often with some kind of crumb coating, batter or sauce. These coatings and sauces generally contain a long list of ingredients, many not natural, which can add significantly to the kilojoule and fat content.

If you're buying frozen seafood from the supermarket, the best options are products with no additives. Plain fish fillets, calamari and prawns (shrimp) are good choices. You can then add flavour at home with fresh herbs, spices or lemon juice. This way you get all the benefits of eating fish without any added nasties: fat, salt or artificial ingredients.

CANNED FISH – A GOOD OPTION?

Canned products are sealed then heat-treated to sterilise them. This gives them a shelf life of up to five years. The low acid content of seafood makes it perfect for microbial growth, so it needs to be treated at a very high temperature to sterilise it. The process preserves the protein and mineral content of the fish, but it compromises heat-sensitive nutrients. Canned tuna, for example, contains lower levels of omega-3s than raw tuna. On a positive note, canned salmon and sardines are good sources of calcium, because we eat the bones, which we wouldn't necessarily do with the fresh fish.

Like most canned products, canned fish and seafood have a time and a place. Canned fish is usually less expensive than fresh, readily available and long-lasting. It's very convenient, ideal to keep on hand for sandwich fillings or quick salads.

Fish can be canned in oil, brine (salt water) or spring water. It's also available with a host of flavourings or sauces. Plain fish in spring water contains the least salt and it contains none of the additives found in the flavoured varieties. Flavoured tuna contains up to four times as much salt as the plain version in spring water.

SMOKED FISH

Smoking is an age-old method of preserving meat, particularly fish. These days, smoking is used more for the unique delicious smoky flavour it provides, rather than for preservation. The fish most commonly smoked are the oily varieties, such as salmon, mackerel, haddock, herring, eel and trout.

Smoked fish contains all the nutrients of fresh fish, including the omega-3 fats. In fact the nutrients are concentrated during smoking, because the fish becomes partially dehydrated. But there are a few health concerns linked to smoked fish (as well as other smoked products and charred meats). The presence of nitrosamines, a by-product of smoking and charring, has been linked to an increased risk of cancer. Consuming smoked fish in moderation, however, is not generally considered a health risk.

Smoked fish also has quite a high salt content, partly because it is salted or brined before smoking. So enjoy smoked fish, like many things, in moderation.

SO HOW CAN I INCLUDE MORE SEAFOOD IN MY DIET?

Seafood is both nutritious and delicious, yet many of us don't reach the target of two serves per week. So what can we do to increase our consumption of this healthy food group? Here are some tips:

- Keep cans of salmon and tuna in the pantry. They make quick, easy, healthy additions to lunchtime salads and sandwiches. Look for the plain varieties in spring water or olive oil.
- Try canned tuna on wholegrain crispbread or sardines on toast for a nutritious and filling snack.
- White-fleshed fish varieties are perfect for young children. They love its mild taste and tend to find it easier to chew and digest than meat.
- Try a seafood version of some of your family favourites. Try prawns (shrimp) or spice-rubbed fish in tacos or burritos, or in a stir-fry with vegetables. Experiment with home-made fish burgers instead of your regular beef burgers.
- Next time you're hosting a barbecue, put fish kebabs on the menu. Whole fresh sardines, salmon cutlets and other oily fish also work well on the barbie, and so do prawns – cook them with the shells on so they don't dry out.
- Buying fresh seafood can be tricky in some regions, especially if you live a long way from the coast. Look for fish fillets, calamari rings or prawns in the freezer section of your supermarket. The plain

uncrumbed versions are the healthiest choices –
you can add your own marinade or spices at home.
- When you do make a trip to the fishmonger or fish
markets, buy extra and freeze some portions.

BUT ISN'T SEAFOOD NOTORIOUSLY DIFFICULT TO COOK?

'Fish is tricky to cook': it's a common misconception.
Nothing could be further from the truth if you choose
one of these dead-easy methods:

- One of my favourite ways to cook fish is in the bag.
Simply place each fish fillet on a large piece of
baking paper, add with some aromatics, such as
fresh herbs, chilli or lemon slices, and fold up
the paper around the fish to make a bag. Roast in
a 200°C (400°F) oven for 15 minutes or steam for
10–12 minutes.
- Roasting is a super-easy way to cook fish. The
trick is to have the oven at a high temperature – say
200– 220°C/400– 425°F). I especially love salmon
cooked this way. As a bonus, you don't get the
cooking smells that you do with pan-frying.
- Barbecuing is ideal for the more robust fish, such as
salmon and tuna. More delicate varieties can also be
barbecued if you wrap them in foil as protection from
the direct heat of the grill.

SHOULD I WORRY ABOUT MERCURY?

Fish and shellfish have a natural tendency to
concentrate mercury in their bodies. Mercury is
harmful to human health if consumed in large
quantities and it can be dangerous to unborn babies.

Most seafood only contains very low levels of
mercury, but predatory fish such as shark, mackerel,
swordfish and tuna generally contain higher levels
than species lower down on the food chain.

Because of their predatory habits, wild-caught fish
generally have higher levels of mercury than farmed
fish, unless the farmed fish have been reared in
contaminated pond or estuary water. The mercury
level of imported fish is subject to government audit
in most countries. Food Standards Australia New
Zealand recommends that as a precaution, pregnant
and breastfeeding women should limit their intake of
fish containing higher mercury levels to 1–2 serves
per fortnight.

TO SUM IT ALL UP

- Seafood is a nutritious addition to your diet and a
valuable source of quality protein as well as many
vitamins and minerals.
- Seafood, particularly oily fish, is a readily available
source of unsaturated omega-3 fatty acids, which
are linked to various health benefits, particularly
heart health.
- To gain the health benefits of eating seafood, aim
for at least 2 serves per week, including a serve
of oily fish.
- Wild-caught and farmed fish are both valuable
sources of nutrition. Wild-caught fish tends to be
slightly lower in calories, while farmed fish is
generally higher in healthy fats.
- Freezing fish is sometimes essential to preserve
its quality. If you're buying packaged frozen fish, be
aware that products without coatings or sauce are
the healthiest choices.
- Canned fish can be convenient and cost-effective,
but is not as nutritious as fresh. Fish canned in
spring water is the best option if you're looking to
minimise added salt and other additives.
- Smoked fish such as salmon and trout are delicious,
but best eaten in moderation.
- All seafood contains mercury and some varieties
contain higher levels than others. If you're pregnant
or breastfeeding, it's safest to eat the high-mercury
varieties no more than once or twice a fortnight.

CITRUS-CURED OCEAN TROUT GRAVLAX
WITH RAW BEETROOT SALAD

This dish makes a great starter and is good for you, too. Ocean trout, like all oily fish, is rich in essential omega-3 fatty acids. The salad of earthy raw beetroot cuts the richness of the trout. The fish takes 24 hours to cure, so leave yourself enough time.

Preparation time: 30 minutes,
    plus 24 hours curing
Cooking time: None
Serves 6 as a starter

2 x 200 g (7 oz) ocean trout fillets,
skin on

2 beetroot (beets), cut into matchsticks

4 small radishes, cut into matchsticks

1 tablespoon chopped dill

2 teaspoons olive oil

2 teaspoons lemon juice

1 tablespoon sunflower seeds,
lightly toasted

CITRUS CURE

160 g (5³/4 oz/¹/2 cup) coarse sea salt

55 g (2 oz/¹/4 cup) caster (superfine)
sugar

2 tablespoons chopped dill

30 ml (1 fl oz) gin

2 teaspoons finely grated lemon zest

2 teaspoons finely grated lime zest

1 teaspoon crushed black peppercorns

Mix together all the ingredients for the citrus cure.

Spread a third of the cure in a large non-metallic dish. Add the trout fillets, skin side down, in a single layer. Spread the rest of the cure over the trout. Cover and refrigerate for 24 hours, turning after 12 hours.

Scrape the cure from the trout, rinse briefly and pat dry with paper towel. Thinly slice the trout on a slight angle, cutting towards the skin (discard the skin).

Mix together the beetroot, radish and dill. Whisk the olive oil and lemon juice in a separate bowl.

To serve, arrange the trout slices, overlapping slightly, on serving plates. Top with the raw beetroot salad, drizzle with the dressing and sprinkle with the toasted sunflower seeds.

✦ TIP ✦
The cured trout will keep, wrapped in plastic, in an airtight container in the fridge for up to 1 week.

CHILLI SQUID SALAD
WITH CUCUMBER, MANGO AND LEMONGRASS

*Grilled or barbecued squid is a low-fat, low-kilojoule source of protein, rich in
B vitamins. Here it's tossed with a spicy Asian salad to make a delicious light meal.*

Preparation time: 25 minutes,
  plus 30 minutes marinating
Cooking time: 5 minutes
Serves 4

600 g (1 lb 5 oz) cleaned baby squid

1 lemongrass stem, white part only,
finely chopped

1 long red chilli, seeded and
finely chopped

1 tablespoon finely chopped coriander
(cilantro) root

1 tablespoon lime juice

2 teaspoons macadamia or peanut oil

2 Lebanese (short) cucumbers

1 large firm ripe mango, diced

150 g (5^1/$_2$ oz) sugar snap peas, sliced

^{1}/$_3$ cup mint leaves

^{1}/$_3$ cup coriander (cilantro) leaves

^{1}/$_3$ cup basil leaves

1 Asian shallot, finely chopped

2 tablespoons unsalted roasted
peanuts, chopped

CHILLI DRESSING

1^1/$_2$ tablespoons lime juice

2 teaspoons fish sauce

2 teaspoons brown sugar

1 long red chilli, seeded and
finely chopped

1 teaspoon finely grated ginger

Cut the squid hoods open and score the insides in a crisscross pattern,
then cut each hood into 3 cm (1 inch) pieces. Mix the lemongrass, chilli,
coriander root, lime juice and oil in a shallow non-metallic dish, add
the squid and stir to coat. Cover and refrigerate for 30 minutes.

Meanwhile, for the chilli dressing, combine the ingredients in a bowl,
stirring to dissolve the sugar.

Cut the cucumbers into long thin ribbons with a peeler, stopping when
you reach the seeds, and place in a large bowl. Add the mango, sugar
snap peas, herbs and shallot.

Heat a large chargrill pan or barbecue plate to high heat. Drain the
squid and grill for 1–2 minutes each side until lightly charred and just
cooked through. Be careful not to overcook or the squid will be tough.

Add half the dressing to the cucumber and toss gently. Serve the salad
topped with grilled squid, drizzled with the remaining dressing and
sprinkled with peanuts.

STEAMED FISH WITH GINGER,
SPRING ONIONS AND SESAME
(see recipe page 154)

FISH AND SWEET POTATO
CAKES WITH DILL DRESSING

(see recipe page 155)

STEAMED FISH
WITH GINGER, SPRING ONIONS AND SESAME

*Super-fast and easy, this dish can be made from any type of firm white fish fillets.
Serve it with lots of steamed greens — bok choy and asparagus, for example — and if
you're extra hungry, add half a cup of steamed brown rice or quinoa per person.*

Preparation time: 5 minutes
Cooking time: 10 minutes
Serves 4

4 x 125 g (4¹/₂ oz) firm white fish fillets
(see tips)

3 cm (1¹/₄ inch) piece ginger,
cut into matchsticks

4 spring onions (scallions), thinly sliced

100 g (3¹/₂ oz) cherry tomatoes, halved

1 tablespoon peanut oil

1 tablespoon low-salt tamari (see tips)

2 teaspoons sesame oil

Steamed Asian greens, to serve

Line a large steamer with baking paper. Add the fish fillets in a single layer and sprinkle with the ginger and spring onions. Arrange the tomatoes on top. Cover and place over a wok or saucepan of simmering water, ensuring the steamer doesn't touch the water. Steam for 6–8 minutes or until the thickest part of the fish flakes easily.

Meanwhile, combine the peanut oil, tamari and sesame oil in a small saucepan and bring to the boil.

Transfer the fish to plates and drizzle with the hot oil. Serve immediately with steamed Asian greens.

✦ TIPS ✦

For a gluten-free version, use gluten-free tamari.

Barramundi and blue eye work well in this recipe.

(pictured page 152)

FISH AND SWEET POTATO CAKES
WITH DILL DRESSING

These fish cakes are made with mashed sweet potato instead of regular potato, and they're coated in wholegrain oats instead of breadcrumbs. I love using sweet potato because it doesn't need any butter or salt to taste great. It has a lower GI than regular potato and it's packed with the powerful antioxidant beta-carotene, which has been linked to a reduced risk of heart disease.

Preparation time: 20 minutes,
   plus 30 minutes chilling
Cooking time: 30 minutes
Serves 4

400 g (14 oz) orange sweet potato, cut into 3 cm (1¼ inch) dice

400 g (14 oz) firm white fish fillets

4 spring onions (scallions), finely chopped

2 tablespoons chopped flat-leaf (Italian) parsley

2 tablespoons chopped dill

1 teaspoon finely grated lemon zest

1 long red chilli, seeded and finely chopped

100 g (3½ oz/1 cup) rolled (porridge) oats

1 tablespoon olive or macadamia oil

Baby English spinach leaves, to serve

DILL DRESSING

1 tablespoon chopped dill

1 tablespoon salted baby capers, rinsed and chopped

1 tablespoon lemon juice

1 tablespoon olive oil

Pinch of caster (superfine) sugar

Steam the sweet potato in a steamer over simmering water for 12 minutes or until tender. Drain, mash roughly with a fork and cool.

Steam the fish in a steamer over simmering water for 6–8 minutes or until just cooked through. Set aside to cool, then flake with a fork.

Combine the sweet potato, fish, spring onion, herbs, lemon zest and chilli in a large bowl. Season with sea salt and freshly ground black pepper. Form the mixture into eight 2 cm (¾ inch) thick patties.

Place the oats on a large plate. Press each fish cake into the oats to coat both sides. Cover and refrigerate for 30 minutes to firm.

Combine all the ingredients for the dill dressing.

Heat the oil in a large frying pan over medium–high heat and cook the fish cakes for 2–3 minutes each side or until golden brown, adding a little extra oil if necessary. Serve with spinach leaves and dill dressing.

✦ TIP ✦
Young children love these fish cakes, but you might need to leave out the chilli.

(pictured page 153)

TUNA TATAKI ON SMASHED AVOCADO
WITH APPLE SALAD AND PONZU DRESSING

Diets rich in omega-3 fatty acids have been linked to a lower risk of cardiovascular disease and also have anti-inflammatory effects. Tuna is a good source of these omega-3s, while the apple salad and ponzu dressing cut through the richness of the fish. This dish is worthy of a dinner party; it's also versatile enough for lunch.

Preparation time: 25 minutes
Cooking time: 1 minute
Serves 4

1 large avocado, diced

2 teaspoons sesame seeds, lightly toasted, plus extra to garnish

3 spring onions (scallions), thinly sliced

2 teaspoons lemon juice

500 g (1 lb 2 oz) piece tuna loin (see tips)

2 teaspoons macadamia or olive oil

75 g (2¾ oz/1½ cups) baby English spinach leaves

25 g (1 oz) beetroot (beet) leaves

1 Lebanese (short) cucumber, seeded and cut into matchsticks

1 green apple, cut into matchsticks (see tips)

PONZU DRESSING

2 tablespoons Japanese soy sauce (see tips)

1 tablespoons lemon juice

1 tablespoon mirin

½ teaspoon finely grated ginger

Whisk together the ponzu dressing ingredients and refrigerate.

Roughly mash the avocado and mix with the toasted sesame seeds, spring onions and lemon juice. Season to taste with sea salt and freshly ground black pepper.

Heat a large chargrill pan or non-stick frying pan over high heat. Brush the tuna with oil and season to taste. Sear the tuna for 20–30 seconds each side. Set aside to cool, then cut into slices.

Mix together the spinach, beetroot leaves, cucumber and apple.

Spread the avocado mixture on plates. Top with the apple salad and tuna slices and drizzle with the ponzu dressing. Garnish with extra toasted sesame seeds.

+ TIPS +

For a gluten-free version, replace the Japanese soy sauce with gluten-free low-salt tamari.

It's important not to overcook the tuna – it should be just seared. Tuna loin can be difficult to obtain. You can replace the loin with four 125 g (4½ oz) tuna steaks.

To prevent the apple discolouring, toss it with a little lemon juice as soon as you cut it.

FISH TACOS WITH SPICED TOMATO AND TOASTED COCONUT SALAD

Spiced fish and a crunchy salad of cucumber, tomato and toasted coconut make these tacos not only delicious but healthy too. The avocado adds creaminess and a good dose of monounsaturated fats. Choose a firm white fish such as blue eye or ling.

Preparation time: 20 minutes
Cooking time: 5 minutes
Serves 4

20 g (3/4 oz/1/3 cup) coconut flakes

1 teaspoon smoked paprika

1/2 teaspoon ground coriander

Pinch of cayenne pepper

1 1/2 tablespoons olive oil

500 g (1 lb 2 oz) firm white fish fillets, cut into 2 cm (3/4 inch) pieces

3 large vine-ripened tomatoes, chopped

2 Lebanese (short) cucumbers, unpeeled, chopped

1/2 firm ripe avocado, diced

1/4 cup coriander (cilantro) leaves, coarsely chopped

1 long red chilli, seeded and finely chopped

Lime juice, to taste, plus lime wedges to serve

8 corn tortillas, warmed

Natural yoghurt, to serve

Heat a large non-stick frying pan over low heat and cook the coconut flakes, stirring, for 2 minutes or until just golden. Set aside to cool.

Combine the paprika, coriander and cayenne pepper and sprinkle evenly over the fish.

Heat 1 tablespoon of the oil in a large non-stick frying pan over medium–high heat and cook the fish, turning, for 2–3 minutes until golden and cooked through.

Toss together the coconut, tomato, cucumber, avocado, coriander and chilli in a large bowl. Add the remaining olive oil and lime juice to taste. Season with sea salt and freshly ground black pepper.

Serve the fish and salad in the warmed tortillas with a wedge of lime and a dollop of yoghurt.

PRAWN, QUINOA AND VEGETABLE STIR-FRY

Quinoa is a great alternative to jasmine rice in Asian stir-fries. It has a lovely nutty taste and it absorbs all the delicious flavours of the stir-fry too. Nutritionally it's superior to rice, with twice as much protein, significantly more dietary fibre and more of the micronutrients potassium, calcium and magnesium.

Preparation time: 20 minutes,
    plus 30 minutes marinating
Cooking time: 25 minutes
Serves 4

1/2 teaspoon chilli flakes

3 garlic cloves, crushed

2 teaspoons finely grated ginger

11/2 tablespoons peanut oil

400 g (14 oz) peeled raw prawns (shrimp), tails intact

150 g (51/2 oz/3/4 cup) quinoa, rinsed

1 large onion, finely chopped

1 bunch asparagus (about 8 spears), sliced

200 g (7 oz) sugar snap peas, sliced

1/2 small red cabbage, shredded

2 tablespoons low-salt tamari (see tips)

Combine the chilli flakes, half the garlic, half the ginger and 2 teaspoons of the oil in a shallow non-metallic dish. Add the prawns and turn to coat well. Cover and refrigerate for 30 minutes.

Meanwhile, put the quinoa with 375 ml (13 fl oz/11/2 cups) cold water in a saucepan over high heat. Bring to the boil, cover, reduce the heat to low and simmer for 12 minutes or until the water has been absorbed and the quinoa is al dente.

Heat 2 teaspoons oil in a large wok or non-stick frying pan over high heat. Stir-fry the prawns for 2–3 minutes until golden and just cooked through; remove from the wok.

Return the wok to high heat, add the remaining oil and stir-fry the onion for 2–3 minutes. Add the remaining garlic and ginger and stir-fry for 1 minute. Add the asparagus, sugar snaps and 2 tablespoons water and stir-fry for 1–2 minutes.

Add the quinoa and cabbage and stir-fry for 1–2 minutes. Add the prawns and tamari and toss for 1 minute to heat through.

✦ TIPS ✦

Prawns are quite high in sodium, but using low-salt tamari keeps the overall sodium content down.

For a gluten-free version, use gluten-free tamari.

BAKED WHOLE SNAPPER WITH
MOROCCAN SPICE PASTE
(see recipe page 164)

BAKED SALMON WITH CRACKED
WHEAT AND GOJI BERRY SALAD
(see recipe page 165)

BAKED WHOLE SNAPPER
WITH MOROCCAN SPICE PASTE

Whole fish are surprisingly easy to cook. A fresh herb and spice paste, too, takes only minutes to make, and it adds a huge amount of flavour. Serve this with lots of steamed Asian greens and some brown rice or quinoa to make a balanced meal.

Preparation time: 15 minutes,
    plus 30 minutes marinating
Cooking time: 25 minutes
Serves 4

½ cup (firmly packed) coriander
(cilantro) leaves, plus extra to garnish

½ cup (firmly packed) mint leaves,
plus extra to garnish

1 long red chilli, seeded and
finely chopped

1 garlic clove

1 teaspoon grated ginger

1 teaspoon ground cumin

1 lemon, thinly sliced,
plus 1 tablespoon lemon juice

2 teaspoons olive oil

1 kg (2 lb 4 oz) whole snapper,
scaled and gutted (see tip)

Finely chop the herbs, chilli, garlic, ginger and cumin in a food processor. Add the lemon juice, olive oil and 1–2 tablespoons water or enough to form a smooth paste. Process until smooth.

Cut three deep diagonal slashes through the skin and down to the bone on each side of the fish. Place the fish in a large non-metallic dish and fill the cavity with the lemon slices. Pour the spice paste over the fish and turn to coat well. Cover and refrigerate for at least 30 minutes.

Preheat the oven to 220°C (425°F). Put the fish on a large paper-lined baking tray and roast for 20–25 minutes or until the thickest part of the flesh flakes easily. Serve garnished with the extra herbs.

✦ TIP ✦

You could use 2 baby snapper (500 g/1 lb 2 oz each) in place of the larger one. The cooking time will decrease to 15–20 minutes.

(pictured page 162)

BAKED SALMON
WITH CRACKED WHEAT AND GOJI BERRY SALAD

This salmon recipe is guaranteed to impress and dead simple to make. Salmon is loaded with healthy fatty acids, while the salad is a good source of dietary fibre.

Preparation time: 30 minutes
Cooking time: 20 minutes
Serves 6

Olive oil spray

750 g (1 lb 10 oz) piece salmon, skin on

1/2 teaspoon sumac

Flat-leaf (Italian) parsley leaves and mint leaves, to garnish

CRACKED WHEAT AND GOJI BERRY SALAD

175 g (6 oz/1 cup) cracked wheat

200 g (7 oz) green beans, sliced

16 asparagus spears, sliced

1/2 cup chopped flat-leaf (Italian) parsley

1/4 cup chopped mint

25 g (1 oz/1/4 cup) goji berries

40 g (11/2 oz/1/4 cup) natural almonds, chopped

2 teaspoons finely grated lemon zest

1 tablespoon lemon juice

1 tablespoon olive oil

1/2 teaspoon sumac

TAHINI DRESSING

190 g (63/4 oz/2/3 cup) natural yoghurt

1 tablespoon tahini

1 tablespoon lemon juice

Preheat the oven to 220°C (425°F).

Put the cracked wheat in a heatproof bowl and pour in enough boiling water to cover it. Soak for 15–20 minutes or until al dente. Drain and press with the back of a spoon to squeeze out the excess moisture. Return the wheat to a large bowl.

Whisk together all the ingredients for the tahini dressing and refrigerate until required.

Cut 2 pieces of foil, each twice the length of the fish. Arrange them on a work surface with the long edges overlapping. Spray with oil. Place the salmon, skin side down, in the centre of the foil. Sprinkle with the sumac. Fold in the edges of the foil to form a parcel. Place on a large baking tray and roast for 15–20 minutes or until cooked to your liking.

Meanwhile, for the cracked wheat and goji berry salad, steam the beans and asparagus for 2 minutes or until just tender. Refresh under cold running water and drain well. Add to the cracked wheat along with the parsley, mint, goji berries, almonds and lemon zest.

Whisk together the lemon juice, olive oil and sumac. Pour over the cracked wheat mixture and gently toss.

Transfer the salmon to a serving platter, drizzle with the tahini dressing and sprinkle with parsley and mint leaves. Serve with the cracked wheat and goji berry salad.

+ **TIP** +

You can use burghul (bulgur) instead of cracked wheat. It is finer than cracked wheat, so it will need only 5 minutes to soak.

(pictured page 163)

MUSSELS WITH TOMATO, CHORIZO AND PAPRIKA

Mussels are low in fat, high in protein and packed with vitamin B₁₂, selenium and magnesium. Chorizo adds a delicious spiciness and depth to the sauce here; it's high in sodium and fat, but you only use a little. You'll need a large heavy-based pan with a tight-fitting lid for this recipe.

Preparation time: 15 minutes
Cooking time: 20 minutes
Serves 4 as a starter

2 teaspoons olive oil

1 red onion, finely chopped

1 small fennel bulb, finely chopped

50 g (1³/4 oz) chorizo, finely diced (see tips)

3 garlic cloves, thinly sliced

1 teaspoon smoked paprika

185 ml (6 fl oz/³/4 cup) white wine

2 large vine-ripened tomatoes, diced

1 kg (2 lb 4 oz) black mussels, scrubbed, beards removed

2 tablespoons chopped flat-leaf (Italian) parsley

Heat the oil in a large heavy-based saucepan over low–medium heat. Add the onion, fennel and chorizo and cook, stirring, for 6–7 minutes or until light golden. Add the garlic and paprika and stir for 1 minute.

Increase the heat to high, add the white wine and simmer until reduced by half. Add the tomatoes and simmer for 1 minute. Add the mussels, cover with a tight-fitting lid and simmer for 6–7 minutes or until the mussels open, shaking the pan occasionally.

Remove from the heat, sprinkle the mussels with the parsley and season with freshly ground black pepper to serve.

+ TIPS +

For a gluten-free version, use gluten-free chorizo.

For a more substantial meal, serve the mussels with a rocket (arugula) salad and some sourdough bread.

MACADAMIA-CRUSTED FISH
WITH GARLIC GREENS

*White fish is an extremely lean source of good-quality protein, yet many of us don't
eat it often enough. In this recipe it's topped with a simple crust — the macadamias
and pepitas add flavour and crunch as well as healthy fats.*

Preparation time: 20 minutes
Cooking time: 15 minutes
Serves 4

75 g (2³/4 oz/¹/2 cup) unsalted raw
macadamia nuts (see tip)

¹/4 cup flat-leaf (Italian) parsley leaves

2 tablespoons pepitas (pumpkin seeds)

2 tablespoons snipped chives

1 garlic clove, crushed, plus 3 extra
cloves, thinly sliced

1 teaspoon finely grated lemon zest

1¹/2 tablespoons lemon juice

4 x 125 g (4¹/2 oz) firm white fish fillets

Olive oil spray

2 teaspoons olive oil

250 g (9 oz) kale, coarsely chopped

¹/4 green cabbage, coarsely chopped

Preheat the oven to 200°C (400°F). Line a large baking tray with
baking paper.

Finely chop the macadamias, parsley, pepitas and chives in a food
processor. Add the crushed garlic, lemon zest and 1 tablespoon lemon
juice and process to a coarse paste, adding 1–2 teaspoons water
if needed.

Press the macadamia mixture onto one side of the fish. Place the fish
on the tray, spray lightly with olive oil and bake for 12 minutes or until
the thickest part of the flesh flakes easily.

Meanwhile, heat the oil in a large wok or non-stick frying pan over
medium–high heat. Stir-fry the sliced garlic for 30 seconds or until
aromatic. Add the kale and cabbage and stir-fry for 2–3 minutes or
until just wilted. Add the remaining lemon juice and season to taste.

Serve the fish on the garlic greens.

+ TIP +
You can replace the macadamias with cashews or almonds.

FROM THE DAIRY

FROM THE DAIRY

Milk, cheese and yoghurt are some of the world's most versatile and widely used foods and they've been around for thousands of years. In Australia we tend to think of dairy products from cow's milk, but local production varies between countries, with some preferring the milk of goats, sheep, buffaloes, horses, yaks, even camels.

ARE DAIRY FOODS GOOD FOR US?

Dairy products are highly nutritious and probably best known for being packed with dietary calcium. Calcium is an essential mineral needed to build strong healthy bones and teeth, prevent osteoporosis, assist muscle and nerve function and help blood clotting.

Dairy products are also an excellent source of protein. The two main types of protein found in cow's milk are casein and whey: both are sources of complete protein, which means they contain all the essential amino acids. They also contain vitamin B_{12}, which plays an important role in the production of red blood cells. The B_{12} content does vary depending upon the type of animal: cow's milk products are a good source of B_{12}, while goat's milk contains much less.

Depending on the product and source of the milk, dairy food is a good source of micronutrients, including vitamins A and D, phosphorous, zinc and magnesium.

HOW MANY SERVES SHOULD WE EAT?

Most guidelines, including Australia's, recommend three serves of dairy per day. Three serves is said to provide most people's daily calcium needs.

AND WHAT IS A SERVE?

- 250 ml (9 fl oz/1 cup) milk
- 40 g (1½ oz) hard cheese (such as cheddar)
- 200 g (7 oz/¾ cup) yoghurt
- 120 g (4¼ oz/½ cup) ricotta cheese
- 250 ml (9 fl oz/1 cup) calcium-fortified milk alternative (at least 100 mg added calcium per 100 ml/3½ fl oz)

WHICH MILK TO CHOOSE?

With so many milks on the market these days, how do you decide which is best for you? Most have a similar protein and calcium content, with the main difference being fat content. Here is a brief run-down of cow's milks:

Skim Also known as nonfat or fat-free milk, skim milk has 0.5 per cent fat, and no saturated fat.

Low-fat Reduced-fat (low-fat) milk has a fat content of 1–2 per cent.

Full-cream Full-cream (whole) milk has a fat content of 3.5 per cent.

A2 All milk contains the A2 milk protein. However, milk branded 'A2' comes from cows whose milk naturally contains *only* the A2 milk protein and is missing the A1 milk protein. Some people report finding it easier to digest. Nutritionally, it's the same.

Lactose-free Lactose-free milk is milk to which an enzyme has been added to break down the lactose into other forms of sugar. It is designed for people who have a lactose intolerance, which means their body does not produce enough of the enzyme lactase to carry out this process naturally during digestion.

Buttermilk Traditionally, buttermilk was a by-product of butter-making, although most of the buttermilk available today is made from milk inoculated with a culture to simulate the taste of the original. It has less than 1 per cent fat and is used mainly in cooking.

Non-homogenised Almost all the milk available in supermarkets has been homogenised. This means it has been passed through fine nozzles under pressure. This makes the fat globules smaller so they are distributed through the milk rather than rising to the top as cream. Non-homogenised milk has not undergone this process. Its nutritional value is the same.

Raw Milk that has not been pasteurised – that is, has not been heated to kill potentially harmful bacteria – is referred to as raw milk. The sale of raw milk for consumption is illegal in Australia because of the associated health risks. It is legal in some other countries, including European Union countries.

Flavoured Flavoured milk is quite high in sugar and it may contain artificial flavours and colours. Plain milk is a healthier choice, as is flavouring your own milk with fruit to make a fruit smoothie.

SO, YOU MIGHT INSTANTLY THINK...

that the milk with the least fat has to be the best choice? Not necessarily so. The saturated fat content in full-cream milk and other dairy products can actually assist satiety (that feeling of fullness) and be more satisfying to consume, meaning you drink or eat less. Some recent studies are also showing evidence that the saturated fat content in dairy foods might not be linked to an increased risk of heart disease, as it's traditionally been thought to be.

But on the flip side, low-fat and skim milk can be good choices for those needing to reduce or control their fat or energy intake for specific health reasons.

I like to drink the full-cream version: it has more flavour, leaves me feeling fuller and is less processed.

WHAT IF I CAN'T DRINK COW'S MILK?

Look in the non-refrigerated milk aisle and you will see that the number of milk alternatives has suddenly tripled. Once limited to soy or rice, there is now an abundance of alternative milks, all claiming to offer different benefits. For those with a dairy or lactose intolerance, and for vegans, these milk alternatives can be a great substitute. For others it is a matter of taste, or comes down to perceived health advantages. Alternative milks can also be used in cooking or for smoothies – each has its own unique flavour to bring to the table. The one thing they generally have in common is they are fortified to varying levels with calcium and often vitamin D.

Here is a run-down of the most widely available dairy milk alternatives:

Soy milk Made from whole soy beans or soy bean protein, soy milk is high in protein and contains no saturated fat. Look for a product made from whole soy beans for the best flavour and the fewest additives. Sugar content varies greatly between brands. Some soy milks contain barley extracts, which means they're not gluten free. Some are fortified with calcium and some are not – check the label.

Almond milk Despite the name, this is nowhere near as nutritious as eating raw almonds – most brands have only around 2 per cent almond content. Almond milk is significantly lower in protein than cow's milk. Some brands are fortified with calcium and vitamin D, others not. Likewise, some contain unwanted sweeteners and other additives. When it comes to almond milk, the most natural option is to make your own, but remember it won't be calcium fortified.

Rice milk Made from brown rice or rice starch, rice milk is lactose free and soy free, so it's suitable for people who want to avoid or can't tolerate those things. It's lower in protein and 'thinner' in texture than cow's milk and doesn't naturally contain much calcium so it needs to be fortified. Some brands are sweetened.

Oat milk Like all plant-based milks, oat milk contains no lactose or cholesterol, but it is also lower in protein and needs to be fortified with calcium.

NAVIGATING THE YOGHURT AISLE

Yoghurt is made by fermenting milk using lactic acid bacteria, which produces the characteristic texture and flavour. Yoghurt can be extremely nutritious, rich in protein, calcium and vitamins D, B_2, B_6 and B_{12}. Yoghurt also contains active bacteria (probiotics) that can help counteract harmful bacteria in the gut and help your immune system. And people with lactose intolerance may tolerate yoghurt better than other dairy products because the lactose is converted to glucose and galactose during fermentation.

Yet the yoghurt aisle can be an absolute minefield. Low-fat, no sugar, no added sugar, skim, extra creamy... the list goes on. Yes, yoghurt in its simplest form is a highly nutritious food. But much of the yoghurt available in supermarkets is highly processed and filled with extra sugar, flavourings and thickeners.

So how do you choose a yoghurt that tastes good and is good for you too? A simple but effective rule of thumb is to look at the ingredients list and choose yoghurt that contains only three, or at the most four, ingredients. Milk, milk solids, live bacteria – and that's it! If the list of ingredients is long, you know the yoghurt contains additives that you really don't need.

The nutritional difference between different types and brands of yoghurt varies according to the type of milk used (whole, reduced-fat or skim), the type of milk solids added before fermentation, the fermentation process and the amount of sugar or fruit added. Here is a run-down of the terms you'll see on labels:

Natural (plain) As the name suggests, this contains no added fruit or sugar and it's available in full-fat and low-fat varieties. Full-fat contains 3–4 per cent fat. It's my personal choice for general use.

Fat free Once again, this sounds like a healthy choice, but it can still be high in sugar. It often contains stabilising agents and thickeners to give it extra body.

Fruit Fruit yoghurt is available in full-fat, low-fat and skim varieties. The fruit gives it about 25–50 per cent more kilojoules, mainly from sugar, than plain varieties with the same fat content. It can contain as much as 20 g (5 teaspoons) sugar per 100 g ($3^{1}/_{2}$ oz).

Sugar free This is the current trend on the market, especially with the recent sugar backlash. Sounds good? Instead of being sweetened with sugar, this generally contains artificial or alternative sweeteners such as stevia. The downside is that artificial sweeteners have been linked to tummy upsets and possible long-term health issues.

Greek-style Thicker and creamier than natural yoghurt and higher in protein, Greek-style yoghurt contains added milk solids or has had some of the whey removed. Full-fat Greek yoghurt contains more fat than natural yoghurt, usually 8–10 per cent. It's ideal to use in desserts.

Pot-set This is fermented in the individual pot in which it's sold, rather than fermented in a big batch, then stirred and poured into pots. It has a firmer texture than stirred yoghurt. In terms of health and nutrition, there's nothing intrinsically better about pot-set yoghurt. However, this method tends to be used to make yoghurt that contains no or few additives, so it's often (although not necessarily) a healthy choice.

Probiotic All yoghurt contains the bacteria *Lactobacillus delbrueckii* subspecies *bulgaricus*, and *Streptococcus salivarius* subspecies *thermophilus*. Probiotic yoghurts contain other live probiotic bacteria as well, such as *Lactobacillus acidophilus*, *Lactobacillus casei* and *Bifidobacterium bifidum*. These are considered to benefit digestion and digestive health and to counteract the negative effects of oral antibiotics.

WHAT ABOUT CHEESE?

Cheese is made by adding a starter culture of bacteria to milk. The bacteria digest the milk sugar (lactose), producing lactic acid. This acidification, plus the addition of rennet, separates the solids (curds) from the liquid (whey, also known as permeate) in the milk. The whey is drained away and the soft curd is pressed to form cheese.

The curd can be eaten fresh, or it can be salted, inoculated with mould, dried or matured according to the type of cheese being made. There are over 300 varieties of cheese, but most can be divided into five broad categories:

- Fresh (unripened) cheeses have a high moisture content and a creamy taste and texture. They have not been aged. Examples include cottage cheese, ricotta, mascarpone and feta.
- Stretched-curd cheeses are the ones that work so well on pizza, such as mozzarella and provolone. The curd is stretched and kneaded in hot water to give it its characteristic stretchiness and texture.
- Semi-soft cheeses are ripened for a relatively short time. Examples include edam, gouda, colby and jack.
- Mould-ripened cheeses are inoculated with a particular strain of mould, either on the surface or throughout the cheese, and then ripened. Examples include brie, camembert, havarti and blue-vein.
- Cooked cheeses are made by cooking the curds to release more whey; the curds are then pressed and aged. These full-flavoured cheeses have a longer shelf life and a drier texture than the mould-ripened and soft cheeses. They also have the most calcium. Examples include cheddar, manchego and parmesan.

SO IS CHEESE A HEALTHY CHOICE?

Nutritionally speaking, cheese is a good source of protein and calcium. It also contains micronutrients including zinc (which supports immunity and healthy skin), vitamin A (essential for healthy vision), vitamin B_2 (which helps the body to convert energy) and vitamin B_{12} (essential for red blood cell production).

Cheese, depending upon its variety, can also be high in fat (especially saturated), cholesterol and salt. Mascarpone, for example, contains over 50 per cent

fat. At the other end of the scale, ricotta and cottage cheese are relatively low-fat.

You can, of course, get reduced-fat varieties of cheese for this very reason. Cheese labelled 'reduced-fat' has 25 per cent less fat than the regular variety, and some low-fat cheeses contain up to 50 per cent less fat than their full-fat equivalents. There's a trade-off, however, in flavour and texture. As with many other foods, I'm a big believer in eating the real stuff, but just eating less of it.

Fresh ricotta is a great healthy choice, being naturally much lower in fat than most cheeses. Look for the fresh version (available by the wedge from delicatessens) rather than the more processed product sold in small tubs – it has a fresher taste and tends to contain less salt.

Parmesan, although high in fat, can be a good choice for cooking. As it's a dry cheese, the flavour is concentrated and you only need a little to get a great flavour kick.

TO SUM IT ALL UP

- Dairy products are a nutritious part of a balanced diet and are excellent sources of calcium, protein, vitamin B_{12} and vitamin D. Aim for 3 serves a day to meet your calcium requirements.
- Full-cream milk is higher in fat than low-fat or skim milk, but it has a better texture and is more satisfying. Reduced-fat milks may suit people who need to watch their kilojoule or fat intake.
- If you prefer to drink one of the many milk alternatives, check the ingredients list for sugar and other additives. Make sure the product has been fortified with calcium and vitamin D.
- When it comes to yoghurt, check the ingredients list. Your yoghurt should not contain more than three or four ingredients. Generally, you can't go wrong with a natural (plain) pot-set yoghurt.
- Cheese is rich in calcium and protein, but some varieties are also high in salt and fat, so should be eaten in moderation.

BREAKFAST POTS
WITH TOASTED OATS AND
VANILLA-POACHED CHERRIES

You can make these breakfast pots in the evening and keep them overnight in the fridge – they'll have more of a bircher muesli consistency but will still be delicious. Greek-style yoghurt is higher in protein than regular natural yoghurt, so it's a good choice for the morning meal. Look for one with no added sugar.

Preparation time: 15 minutes,
   plus chilling
Cooking time: 15 minutes
Serves 4

80 ml (2½ fl oz/⅓ cup) cranberry juice

1 tablespoon honey or maple syrup

1 teaspoon vanilla bean paste

450 g (1 lb/3 cups) cherries, pitted (see tips)

70 g (2½ oz/⅔ cup) rolled (porridge) oats

2 tablespoons sunflower seeds

1 tablespoon linseeds (flaxseeds)

1 teaspoon ground cinnamon

520 g (1 lb 2¾ oz/2 cups) Greek-style or thick sheep's milk yoghurt

Combine the cranberry juice, honey and vanilla in a saucepan and bring to the boil over high heat. Reduce the heat and simmer for 2–3 minutes until reduced by half. Add the cherries, remove from the heat and leave to cool. Transfer to a bowl, cover and refrigerate.

Preheat the oven to 180°C (350°F). Line a large baking tray with baking paper. Combine the oats, sunflower seeds, linseeds and cinnamon, spread on the tray and bake for 5–7 minutes until golden. Leave to cool.

Spoon the yoghurt, oat mixture and cherries into glasses in layers, finishing with some poached cherries.

✦ TIPS ✦

When cherries are out of season you can use frozen instead, or substitute strawberries.

These pots will keep, covered, in the fridge for up to 2 days.

SPINACH AND CAPSICUM MUFFINS
WITH VINTAGE CHEDDAR

Spelt flour is ground from an ancient variety of wheat. I like to use it for baking because it's higher in protein and fibre than regular wheat flour and gentler on the digestive system. Use a sharp vintage cheese to give these muffins lots of flavour.

Preparation time: 15 minutes
Cooking time: 20 minutes
Makes 12

300 g (10^1/$_2$ oz/2 cups) spelt flour (see tips)

3 teaspoons baking powder

150 g (5^1/$_2$ oz) baby English spinach leaves

1 cob corn, kernels removed

75 g (2^3/$_4$ oz) roasted red capsicum (pepper), diced

70 g (2^1/$_2$ oz/^{2}/$_3$ cup) grated vintage cheddar cheese (see tips)

250 ml (9 fl oz/1 cup) buttermilk

2 eggs

60 ml (2 fl oz/^{1}/$_4$ cup) macadamia oil or melted unsalted butter

Preheat the oven to 190°C (375°F). Line a 12-hole 125 ml (4 fl oz/^{1}/$_2$ cup) muffin tin with paper cases. Sift the flour and baking powder into a large bowl.

Put the spinach in a bowl or pan, cover with boiling water, then drain, refresh under cold water and drain again. Squeeze out the water and finely chop.

Add the spinach, corn, capsicum and cheese to the flour mixture. Whisk the buttermilk, eggs and oil together, add to the dry ingredients and stir until just combined (don't overmix).

Spoon into the muffin cases and bake for 18–20 minutes until golden.

✦ TIPS ✦

For a vegetarian version, use cheddar made without animal rennet.

You can use either wholegrain or white spelt flour in this recipe.

The muffins are best eaten on the day of baking, but they also freeze well. Let them cool completely, then wrap individually in plastic wrap and freeze for up to 2 months.

SPICED SWEET POTATO DIP

Natural yoghurt makes the ideal base for rich, creamy dips and contains only a fraction of the fat of cream cheese. In this dip, carrot or pumpkin works just as well as sweet potato. Serve the dip with vegetable sticks or pitta crisps, or use it as a spread on sandwiches.

Preparation time: 10 minutes
Cooking time: 5 minutes
Makes about 500 g (1 lb 2 oz/2 cups)

2 teaspoons olive oil

2 garlic cloves, crushed

1 teaspoon ground cumin

1 teaspoon ground coriander

250 g (9 oz) sweet potato, grated

260 g (9¼ oz/1 cup) natural yoghurt

2 tablespoons chopped coriander (cilantro) leaves

2 teaspoons lemon juice

2 teaspoons tahini

Vegetable sticks or pitta crisps, to serve

Heat the olive oil in a large non-stick frying pan over medium heat. Add the garlic, cumin and ground coriander and cook, stirring, for 1 minute or until fragrant.

Add the sweet potato and stir for 3–4 minutes until tender. Remove from the heat and leave to cool completely.

Combine the sweet potato mixture, yoghurt, coriander, lemon juice and tahini in a large bowl and season to taste with sea salt and freshly ground black pepper. Serve with vegetable sticks or pitta crisps.

+ TIP +

The dip will keep in an airtight container in the fridge for up to 4 days.

LABNE

Labne is a 'cheese' made from strained yoghurt. Like yoghurt, it has a delicious tangy flavour and smooth, creamy consistency, and it's lower in fat than most cheeses. Making your own is surprisingly simple – the trick is to use really good-quality pot-set natural yoghurt with nothing added. Spread the labne on crostini, use it as a dip, or add it to salads as you would feta.

Preparation time: 20 minutes,
  plus 48–72 hours draining
Cooking time: None
Makes 500–600 g (1 lb 2 oz–1 lb 5 oz)

1 kg (2 lb 4 oz) pot-set full-cream natural yoghurt

2 teaspoons sea salt

½ cup finely chopped herbs (see tips)

Olive oil, to cover

Mix together the yoghurt and salt. Line a large sieve with muslin (cheesecloth) and place over a large bowl. Spoon the yoghurt into the lined sieve.

Cover and refrigerate for 48–72 hours (see tips). After this time, the whey from the yoghurt will have drained into the bowl and the yoghurt should be thick enough to roll into balls.

Spread the herbs on a large plate. Roll tablespoons of yoghurt into balls, then carefully roll them in herbs to coat. Place them in a 500 ml (17 fl oz/2 cup) sterilised jar (see tips). Add enough olive oil to cover the balls. Cover and keep in the refrigerator for up to 1 month.

+ TIPS +

Parsley, thyme, basil or mint work well in this recipe.

You'll need to drain the yoghurt for at least 48 hours. After 24 hours, it will have a dip-like consistency, but it will continue to thicken as more whey drains away.

To sterilise the jar, simply put it through the hot cycle in a dishwasher. Alternatively, wash and rinse it thoroughly, then heat it in the oven at 160°C (315°F) for 20 minutes. Cool completely before using.

CROSTINI WITH MARINATED LABNE
AND TWO TOPPINGS

Creamy labne makes a delicious starting point for crostini toppings such as raw marinated zucchini, or salty prosciutto with tart fresh plums.

Preparation time: 15 minutes
Cooking time: 5 minutes
Serves 4 as a starter

8 thin slices rye or wholegrain sourdough bread

60 g (2¼ oz/½ cup) drained labne (see recipe page 179)

Olive oil, for drizzling

MARINATED ZUCCHINI TOPPING

2 zucchini (courgettes)

1 tablespoon white balsamic vinegar

1 tablespoon olive oil

1 teaspoon finely grated lemon zest

¼ cup mint leaves, coarsely chopped (optional)

PROSCIUTTO, PLUM AND HAZELNUT TOPPING

4 thin slices prosciutto, coarsely torn

2 plums, thinly sliced (see tip)

2 tablespoons lightly toasted hazelnuts, peeled and coarsely chopped (see page 19)

To make the marinated zucchini topping, cut long ribbons from the zucchini with a vegetable peeler, stopping when you reach the seeds.

Whisk together the vinegar, olive oil and lemon zest in a large bowl. Add the zucchini and mint and toss gently. Season with sea salt and black pepper. Leave for 5 minutes for the flavours to develop.

Toast the bread and spread with labne. Top half the slices with prosciutto, plum slices and toasted hazelnuts and the other half with marinated zucchini. Drizzle with a little olive oil and serve immediately.

✦ TIP ✦

When plums are out of season, substitute a thinly sliced pear.

BAKED RICOTTA
WITH HERB, TOMATO AND WALNUT SALAD

I love ricotta for its creamy taste and especially as it contains only a fraction of the fat of most cheeses. Baked, it makes a wonderful shared starter and it's perfect for picnics too. Spread it on toast or serve sliced as part of an antipasto platter.

Preparation time: 20 minutes
Cooking time: 30 minutes
Serves 8–10 as a starter

Olive oil spray

500 g (1 lb 2 oz) fresh ricotta cheese (see tips)

2 eggs, lightly beaten

35 g (1¼ oz/⅓ cup) grated parmesan cheese (see tips)

40 g (1½ oz/⅓ cup) pitted black olives, chopped

2 tablespoons chopped basil

2 tablespoons chopped flat-leaf (Italian) parsley, plus 2 tablespoons parsley leaves

¼ teaspoon dried chilli flakes

1 tablespoon olive oil

100 g (3½ oz) grape or cherry tomatoes, chopped

2 tablespoons mint leaves

2 tablespoons oregano leaves

2 tablespoons walnuts, lightly toasted and coarsely chopped

Grilled bread, to serve (see tips)

Preheat the oven to 160°C (315°F). Spray a 10 x 20 cm (4 x 8 inch) non-stick loaf (bar) tin with oil.

Mix the ricotta, eggs and parmesan in a food processor until smooth. Transfer to a large bowl, stir in the olives, basil and chopped parsley, and season with sea salt and black pepper. Spoon into the tin and bake for 25 minutes or until golden around the edges and set.

Line a large baking tray with baking paper. Carefully turn out the ricotta onto the tray. Sprinkle with chilli flakes and drizzle with 2 teaspoons of the olive oil. Return to the oven for 5 minutes, then leave to cool for 10 minutes.

Meanwhile, combine the tomatoes, remaining parsley, mint, oregano and toasted walnuts. Add the remaining olive oil and season to taste.

Serve the ricotta with the tomato salad over the top and some slices of grilled bread.

+ TIPS +

For a vegetarian version, use parmesan made without animal rennet.

The recipe is gluten free if you serve with gluten-free bread.

It's important to use fresh ricotta, available from delicatessens and the deli section of supermarkets. It has a much firmer texture than the ricotta sold pre-packaged in small tubs.

QUINOA-CRUSTED CHEESE TARTS
WITH PUMPKIN AND CRISP SAGE

Unlike traditional pastry, a quinoa crust is super-healthy – it provides a good dose of protein, fibre, manganese and phosphorous. Roasted pumpkin is naturally sweet, perfect in this tangy blue-cheese filling.

Preparation time: 30 minutes
Cooking time: 1 hour
Makes 4

150 g (5$^{1}/_{2}$ oz/$^{3}/_{4}$ cup) quinoa, rinsed

375 ml (13 fl oz/1$^{1}/_{2}$ cups) home-made or low-salt vegetable stock

500 g (1 lb 2 oz) peeled and seeded pumpkin (winter squash), diced (see tips)

1 tablespoon chopped sage, plus small sage leaves to garnish

2 teaspoons honey

1 tablespoon olive oil

35 g (1$^{1}/_{4}$ oz/$^{1}/_{3}$ cup) finely grated parmesan cheese (see tips)

1 egg, plus 1 egg white

Olive oil spray

$^{1}/_{4}$ cup chopped herbs, such as chives and parsley

130 g (4$^{1}/_{2}$ oz) fresh ricotta cheese

75 g (2$^{3}/_{4}$ oz) blue cheese, crumbled (see tips)

Place the quinoa and stock in a small saucepan and bring to the boil. Reduce the heat to low, cover and simmer for 12 minutes or until the stock has been absorbed. Set aside to cool.

Meanwhile, preheat the oven to 180°C (350°F) and line a large tray with baking paper. Combine the pumpkin with the chopped sage, honey and 2 teaspoons of the oil and spread over the tray. Season with sea salt and freshly ground pepper and roast for 25–30 minutes until tender.

Mix together the quinoa, parmesan, egg and white and season well.

Lightly spray four 12 cm (4$^{1}/_{2}$ inch) round non-stick fluted tart tins with oil (see tips). Press the quinoa mixture firmly into the tins to form a thick crust. Place on a large baking tray and bake for 15 minutes or until light golden.

Mix together the ricotta and blue cheese and spread a little into each tart crust. Top with the roasted pumpkin and bake for 3–4 minutes to warm through.

Meanwhile, heat the remaining oil in a small saucepan over medium–high heat. Add the sage leaves and stir for 1–2 minutes until crisp. Drain on paper towel. Serve the tarts topped with crisp sage leaves.

+ TIPS +

This recipe is vegetarian if you use parmesan and blue cheeses made with non-animal rennet.

You will need about 750 g (1 lb 10 oz) pumpkin with the rind on to yield 500 g (1 lb 2 oz) flesh.

Be sure to use well-greased non-stick tart tins or the crusts will stick.

LAMB AND HALOUMI SKEWERS
WITH LENTIL AND SILVERBEET SALAD

Haloumi is a delicious firm cheese originating from Cyprus. It holds its shape well when cooked, but it does tend to be very salty, so look for a salt-reduced variety. I love raw silverbeet in salads, although you could use kale or English spinach instead here – all are rich sources of vitamin K, vitamin C, fibre and folate. You'll need eight skewers: if you use wooden ones, soak them in cold water for 20 minutes first, to prevent them from burning.

Preparation time: 25 minutes,
   plus 30 minutes marinating
Cooking time: 5 minutes
Serves 4

1¹/₂ tablespoons olive oil

1¹/₂ tablespoons lemon juice

1 garlic clove, crushed

1 teaspoon dried mint

400 g (14 oz) lamb leg steaks,
cut into 1.5 cm (¹/₂ inch) dice

150 g (5¹/₂ oz) low-salt haloumi,
cut into 1.5 cm (⁵/₈ inch) dice

2 teaspoons balsamic vinegar

1 teaspoon dijon mustard

400 g (14 oz) can brown lentils, rinsed

2 celery stalks, diced

¹/₂ red onion, finely chopped

250 g (9 oz) silverbeet (Swiss chard),
centre vein removed, chopped

200 g (7 oz) red and yellow grape
tomatoes, halved

Lemon wedges, to serve

Combine 1 tablespoon of the olive oil, 1 tablespoon of lemon juice, the garlic and the mint in a shallow non-metallic dish. Add the lamb and turn to coat well. Leave to marinate in the fridge for at least 30 minutes.

Thread the lamb and haloumi alternately onto 8 skewers.

Cook the skewers in a large chargrill pan or non-stick frying pan over medium–high heat for 4–5 minutes or until cooked to your liking. Transfer to a plate, cover loosely with foil and leave for 2–3 minutes.

Whisk the remaining olive oil, remaining lemon juice, vinegar and mustard in a large bowl. Add the lentils, celery and onion and toss gently. Set aside for 5 minutes for the flavours to develop. Stir in the silverbeet and tomatoes and season with sea salt and black pepper.

Serve the skewers on the salad with a wedge of lemon.

ORANGE, SAFFRON AND
DATE CUSTARDS
(see recipe page 190)

ROASTED STRAWBERRIES WITH
ROSEWATER, RICOTTA-YOGHURT
CREAM AND PISTACHIOS
(see recipe page 191)

ORANGE, SAFFRON AND DATE CUSTARDS

Shop-bought custard can't be compared with home-made — most commercial versions don't even contain eggs. These little baked beauties made from eggs and whole milk are a good source of protein and calcium and they have a naturally sweet surprise at the bottom: caramel-textured dates. Look for pure maple syrup and avoid the artificial 'maple flavoured' products.

Preparation time: 15 minutes
Cooking time: 30 minutes
Makes 4

400 ml (14 fl oz) full-cream milk (see tip)

2 tablespoons pure maple syrup

Pinch of saffron strands

1 egg

3 egg yolks

Finely grated zest of 1 orange

75 g (2³/4 oz/about 3) medjool dates, pitted and diced

Orange segments, to serve

Preheat the oven to 160°C (315°F). Combine the milk, maple syrup and saffron in a saucepan and stir over low heat until at simmering point.

Meanwhile, place the egg, egg yolks and orange zest in a large bowl. Whisk with a fork until well combined (do not overmix). Gradually stir in the hot milk mixture.

Divide the dates between four 125 ml (4 fl oz/¹/2 cup) ovenproof ramekins. Place the ramekins in a large deep roasting tin. Pour the custard into the ramekins. Pour boiling water into the roasting tin to come halfway up the sides of the ramekins.

Bake for 20–25 minutes or until the custards are set but still have a definite wobble in the centre. Leave to cool slightly before serving warm or chilled. Top with orange segments just before serving.

✦ TIP ✦

For a dairy-free version, use soy milk. For a truly rich and decadent custard, replace half the milk with pure cream.

(pictured page 188)

ROASTED STRAWBERRIES
WITH ROSEWATER, RICOTTA-YOGHURT CREAM AND PISTACHIOS

Strawberries take only minutes to roast and release their delicious juices. The combination of ricotta and natural yoghurt in this recipe is healthier than cream or mascarpone, but it still has a rich, creamy texture.

Preparation time: 10 minutes
Cooking time: 10 minutes
Serves 4

500 g (1 lb 2 oz) strawberries, hulled and halved

Few drops of rosewater (see tip)

1 1/2 tablespoons pure floral honey

240 g (8 1/2 oz/1 cup) fresh ricotta cheese

200 g (7 oz/3/4 cup) Greek-style or thick natural yoghurt

1 teaspoon vanilla bean paste

1/2 teaspoon ground cinnamon

Chopped pistachios, to garnish

Preheat the oven to 180°C (350°F). Place the strawberries in a large roasting dish and drizzle with the rosewater and 2 teaspoons of the honey. Roast for 5–10 minutes or until just soft. Set aside to cool.

Whisk together the remaining honey and the ricotta, yoghurt, vanilla and cinnamon. Spoon into glasses, top with the strawberries and garnish with pistachios.

+ **TIP** +

Rosewater is available from delicatessens and Middle Eastern grocery stores.

(pictured page 189)

FROM THE ORCHARD

FROM THE ORCHARD

Sweet, juicy and totally delicious, fresh fruit really is nature's answer to sugar. Their botanical definition is complex, but we generally use the term 'fruit' to refer to the fleshy edible parts of flowering plants. They can be eaten raw, frozen, canned, dried or juiced, or even turned into jams and preserves.

IS FRUIT GOOD FOR US?

Of course it is! Just like vegetables, fruit is extremely nutritious, being rich in:

- Vitamin C, a powerful antioxidant that helps wounds heal and aids iron absorption
- Dietary fibre, essential for digestive health. Fruit is rich in both soluble and insoluble fibre, as well as pectin, a type of soluble fibre which can help maintain healthy levels of cholesterol
- Potassium, essential for fluid balance; it also assists muscle function and metabolism
- Beta carotene, important for healthy eyes and skin
- B vitamins, essential for energy metabolism, growth and hormone function

With a water content of 70–90 per cent, fresh fruit is low in kilojoules, low in protein and, with the exception of avocados and olives, contains no saturated fats. It is a good source of natural sugars, providing quick energy, and rich in disease-fighting antioxidants and polyphenols. Antioxidants help prevent our body's cells from being damaged by unstable free radicals. Some polyphenols have the same effect and are thought to have a role in reducing inflammation and preventing diseases such as cancer and cardiovascular disease.

HOW MUCH FRUIT SHOULD WE EAT?

The World Health Organization recommends a minimum of 400 g (14 oz) fruit and vegetables per day to help prevent chronic diseases and micronutrient deficiencies. Australia's dietary guidelines recommend two to three serves of fruit per day.

AND WHAT IS A SERVE?

- 1 'medium' fruit, such as an apple, banana or pear
- 2 'small' fruits, such as apricots or plums
- 1 cup diced fruit such as watermelon or pineapple
- 1 cup canned fruit (with no added sugar)
- 30 g (1 oz) dried fruit, such as sultanas, apricots or dates (eat only occasionally)
- 125 ml (4 fl oz/1/2 cup) fresh fruit juice

HOW FRESH IS 'FRESH'?

Most fresh fruits have a limited season, so if they're available out of season in your local supermarket, they've either come from another region with a different climate or they've been kept in cold storage. Cold storage allows fruit to be sold long after picking. Apples are a great example – available all year round, they're actually harvested for only three months.

Apples from cold storage have been held in conditions where temperature, humidity, oxygen and carbon dioxide levels are carefully controlled. The aim is to prevent full ripening and slow down deterioration. The fruit is, in effect, put to sleep. Sometimes the fruit is treated with chemicals (such as 1-methylcyclopropene) to temporarily stop some of the biochemical changes that would otherwise cause it to ripen.

The nutritional value of fruit from cold storage is generally similar to that of fresh fruit, but flavour, texture and shelf life can be greatly compromised.

Cold-stored fruit is sometimes also sprayed with fungicides to prevent mould, but the use of chemicals in the food chain is tightly controlled. Imported fruit and vegetables are usually fumigated with methyl bromide to comply with quarantine regulations.

DRIED FRUIT IS GOOD FOR ME, RIGHT?

These intensely sweet small packages certainly pack a flavour punch, but are they good for us?

Drying fruit evolved as a method of preserving. Excess fruit left over from the harvest could be dried rather than wasted – then seasonal fruits could be eaten in their dried form all year round.

Dried fruits have had their moisture removed either by the sun or in specialised dryers and dehydrators. This results in a product that is very low in moisture and high in sugar, which means it has a long shelf life – much longer than fresh fruit.

Dried fruit, then, is an extremely concentrated form of energy and nutrients. For example, two dried apricot halves contain essentially the same nutrients as a fresh apricot (other than vitamin C). The water loss means greatly reduced volume and yet the nutrients, kilojoules and sugar are more concentrated, making dried apricots a highly flavoured, energy-dense snack in a small package.

To put that into perspective, have a look at the chart below and consider this: you probably wouldn't eat five fresh apricots in one sitting, but you'd happily munch on the equivalent dried amount – about 10 dried apricot halves – and not think much of it, despite all the kilojoules and sugar.

Dried fruit can be a valuable source of energy, especially for athletes or for anyone enjoying endurance activities. But for everyday life, dried fruit should really be eaten only in moderation, because in terms of its sugar and kilojoule count it's not unlike sweets. It does, however, provide the benefit of a great whack of dietary fibre and nutrients that sweets don't contain.

...AND THE DOWNSIDE

Sulphur dioxide (220) is a food additive that's often used as an antioxidant in dried fruit (particularly raisins, apples, peaches and apricots) to preserve their colour and flavour. It works by blocking the oxidative reactions that would otherwise darken the fruit. You can easily identify fruit that has been dried without sulphur dioxide, because it tends to be darker brown in colour, be less 'perfect' looking and have a stronger flavour.

Sulphites such as sulphur dioxide can be problematic for asthmatics (causing increased symptoms or attacks), as well as causing stomach upsets, headaches or diarrhoea for those with a sensitivity. Sulphur dioxide is generally harmless for non-asthmatics, but if I can avoid it I usually do, just as I try to avoid other additives. Dried fruit without sulphur dioxide can be found in health-food stores. Certified organic dried fruit doesn't have sulphur dioxide added.

Dried fruit is already packed with natural sugar, but some brands have even more sugar added. Some to look out for are dried pineapple (often coated in sugar), dried banana chips (deep-fried and then sweetened with sugar) and dried cranberries, which have sugar added to counteract their natural tartness.

Dried fruit bars are often touted as a 'health food', especially for children, and are often put into lunch boxes as a 'healthy snack'. The reality is that many are highly processed, contain a host of additives, including a lot of sugar, and aren't particularly nutritious. In its purest form a dried fruit bar should contain just fruit (no added sugar, salt or fillers) and be considered a 'sweet treat', not a serve of fruit.

	KJ (CAL)	WATER (%)	FIBRE (G)	SUGAR (G)	PROTEIN (G)
Fresh apricots (100 g/3½ oz)	171 (40)	86	2.5	6.6	0.8
Dried apricots (100 g/3½ oz)	886 (211)	30	8.4	40.5	4.3

FRESH OR CANNED?

Nothing beats fresh when it comes to taste, flavour and texture. But when your favourite fruit is out of season, canned definitely has a place.

Once harvested, fresh fruit begins to lose its nutritive value. And the longer the time between harvest and eating, the bigger the decrease in nutrients. Likewise, if fruit is not stored correctly, at the right temperature, or has to travel long distances, this process can occur quite rapidly.

Canned fruit is picked at the peak of its ripeness and then processed right away. The canning process does, however, involve heat, so heat-sensitive nutrients such as vitamin C are destroyed. On the plus side, the fruit is processed when it's very fresh, so nutrients not sensitive to heat, such as potassium and vitamin A, are retained and their levels can in fact be higher than in fresh fruit.

Additives are an issue, as they are in many processed foods. Some fruit is canned in syrup, which is loaded with sugar. To avoid the extra sugar and kilojoules, look for fruit canned in water or natural juice. Some fruit is now being packed in 'sweetened water'. This means alternative or artificial sweeteners are used to replace the sugar – not ideal.

Another consideration is that many fruits – peaches and pears, for example – are peeled before canning. Removing the skin means removing most of the dietary fibre, which is one of the nutritional benefits of fruit.

FABULOUSLY FROZEN?

Many fruits are available in the freezer section of the supermarket, especially those with a short season, such as berries, cherries and mangoes. Frozen fruits are snap-frozen immediately after harvest, so nutritionally speaking they are comparable to fresh produce. In fact, frozen fruit can come out in front of fresh fruit that is more than a day or two old. You lose out on texture, but for baking or smoothies, frozen fruit is a staple in my freezer. Another benefit is that the price is consistent year-round and there is no wastage.

BUT WHAT ABOUT FRUIT JUICES?

Personally, I've never been a fan of fruit juices. Like dried fruits, they make it easy to consume a lot of sugar and kilojoules without realising it. A glass of orange juice, for example, might contain five oranges. So, that's the sugar and kilojoules of five pieces of fruit. But you'd be unlikely to eat your way through five whole oranges in one sitting.

As always, fresh is best. Juicing your own fruit is by far the most nutritious choice. But remember that most domestic juicers leave the skin behind, so you miss out on most of the dietary fibre. Adding some veggies to your fruit juice is a great way to reduce the overall sugar and kilojoule content and also sneak in one of your daily serves of vegetables.

Almost every fruit seems to be available now from the supermarket in some sort of juice format – fresh, processed, concentrated, diluted, with or without additives. So how do you know which is the healthiest choice? Here's a breakdown for next time you're trying to navigate the juice aisle:

Fresh squeezed Juice that has been extracted then bottled without pasteurisation or additives.

Concentrate Juice that has been pasteurised, filtered, reduced by heating and evaporation, then stored and transported in concentrate form. Essences, oils and vitamin C removed during the process may be added to restore flavour. Water is added to reconstitute the juice to close to its original form and nutritive value.

Not from concentrate The juice is pasteurised and stored in oxygen-depleted tanks to prevent spoilage. It can be stored this way for up to a year before it is packaged. The process removes most of the flavour and aroma associated with fresh juice, so 'flavour packs' are added to restore what was lost during processing. Flavour packs are derived from orange peel and may contain other additives, including ethyl butyrate, a natural aroma, to give a 'fresh squeezed' taste. Scary, huh?

Fruit juice drink A diluted juice product that may contain as little as 5 per cent fruit juice, from concentrate. (Most fruit juice drinks contain 15–30 per cent juice.) The remainder of the drink is made up of water, sugar or artificial sweetener, and flavouring. Some fruit juice drinks contain as much as 8–10 teaspoons of sugar in a 350 ml (12 fl oz) pack – similar to sugary soft drinks such as Coca-Cola.

Other additives Citric acid or ascorbic acid is often added to improve taste, and vitamin C may be added to replace what's been destroyed during pasteurisation.

THE F WORD

I'm talking about fructose! Fructose is a naturally occurring sugar found in modest amounts in fresh fruit. It also occurs naturally in vegetables and honey.

Crystalline fructose is a processed form of fructose, made by processing cane sugar (which is 50 per cent fructose), sugar beet or corn.

High-fructose corn syrup is another processed form of fructose. It is made by milling corn into starch, processing the starch to form glucose syrup, and adding enzymes that convert some of the glucose into fructose. (Despite its name, it is lower in fructose than crystalline fructose.)

Crystalline fructose and high-fructose corn syrup are both commonly used as low-cost sweeteners in a whole array of drinks, confectionery, packaged baked goods, snack foods and breakfast cereals.

In the human body, fructose is converted into glucose, which is then stored in the liver or muscles to be used as an on-demand energy source. If the body is already overloaded with glucose, it converts the fructose to triglycerides (fat).

Fructose is often dubbed the evil ingredient in Western societies, a major contributor to the obesity crisis. Without a doubt, processed fructose is creeping into a lot of processed foods, and the overall sugar intake of many people has gone through the roof. But it's our *total* sugar intake that we need to address.

The natural fructose found in fruit makes up very little of our total sugar intake, while fruit provides a host of other benefits, such as fibre, nutrients and antioxidants. Consuming fructose in its natural form – fresh fruit – in moderation will not make you overweight. Consuming large amounts of highly processed food loaded with processed fructose, on the other hand, means consuming a lot of kilojoules, and it's this that contributes to weight gain.

TO SUM IT ALL UP

- Fruit is an extremely nutritious food, low in kilojoules, high in fibre, vitamin C and potassium, and loaded with antioxidants. We should aim to eat two to three serves per day.
- Canned and frozen fruit can be good choices when fruit is expensive or not in season. Always choose canned fruit in natural juice or water, and remember, the fibre content will be lower if the fruit has been peeled. Use frozen fruit for baking and smoothies.
- Dried fruit is a concentrated source of nutrients, sugar and energy, so should be eaten in moderation. Choose dried fruit that hasn't been treated by sulphur dioxide if possible.
- Fruit juice is a food and should never be a replacement for drinking water. One 'serve' of fruit juice is just half a cupful. Juicing your own fruit is the best choice, nutritionally, but the healthiest packaged juice is the one labelled 'fresh squeezed', with no added sugar.
- Fructose is the naturally occurring sugar found in fruit and shouldn't be confused with processed forms of fructose that exist in many processed foods.

BERRY SMOOTHIE
WITH AVOCADO AND COCONUT WATER

Smoothies are often based on fruit juice, but I like to use coconut water instead to keep the sugar levels down.

Preparation time: 5 minutes
Cooking time: None
Serves 2 for breakfast

400 ml (14 fl oz) coconut water

195 g (7 oz/1$\frac{1}{2}$ cups) frozen mixed berries (see tips)

$\frac{1}{2}$ avocado, chopped

1 tablespoon LSA (linseed, sunflower seed and almond meal) blend (see tips)

Combine all the ingredients in a blender and blend on high speed until smooth. Serve immediately.

✦ TIPS ✦

Frozen berries are often more convenient and they actually work better than fresh here, resulting in a thick, cold smoothie.

LSA blend is available from the health-food section of supermarkets.

GREEN ZING SMOOTHIE
WITH MANGO AND CHIA

Green smoothies are a great way to add a serve of vegetables to your daily intake. Mint or coriander adds freshness, while the chia will help keep you feeling full.

Preparation time: 5 minutes
Cooking time: None
Serves 2 for breakfast

400 ml (14 fl oz) coconut water

270 g (9$\frac{1}{2}$ oz/1$\frac{1}{2}$ cups) seedless green grapes

1 large mango, chopped (see tip)

30 g (1 oz/$\frac{2}{3}$ cup) baby English spinach or kale leaves

$\frac{1}{4}$ cup coriander (cilantro) or mint leaves

1 tablespoon chia seeds

Handful of ice cubes

Combine all the ingredients in a blender and blend on high speed until smooth and thick. Serve immediately.

✦ TIP ✦

When mango is out of season, replace it with any other fresh fruit – bananas or kiwi fruit work well.

CITRUS SALAD
WITH YOGHURT, POMEGRANATE AND MINT

This salad makes a light, refreshing breakfast or dessert when citrus fruits are in season. Feel free to add a handful of chopped nuts or seeds for protein. The sugar counteracts the tartness of the fruit, but you can leave it out if you prefer.

Preparation time: 10 minutes
Cooking time: None
Serves 2 for breakfast

2 ruby red grapefruit

2 navel oranges or blood oranges

1 lime

1 teaspoon brown or coconut sugar

1 tablespoon pomegranate seeds

2 tablespoons small mint leaves

130 g (4½ oz/½ cup) Greek-style or thick coconut yoghurt

Remove the skin and pith from the citrus fruit using a small sharp knife. Slice the fruit into thin rounds and arrange on serving plates.

Sprinkle with sugar and top with pomegranate seeds and mint. Serve with yoghurt.

+ TIP +
This salad is vegan if you use coconut yoghurt.

FIG, WATERCRESS AND ASPARAGUS SALAD
WITH GOAT'S CHEESE TOASTS

Fresh figs are totally delicious and versatile too – they work equally well in sweet and savoury dishes. Look for firm figs with no blemishes and use them within a day or two of purchasing.

Preparation time: 15 minutes
Cooking time: 15 minutes
Serves 4 as a starter or light meal

2 bunches asparagus (about 16 spears)

1 tablespoon olive oil

6 figs, halved (see tips)

4 slices prosciutto (optional), torn

75 g (2³/4 oz/4 cups) watercress leaves

2 tablespoons snipped chives

1 tablespoon red wine vinegar

1 French shallot, finely chopped

8 slices rye or wholegrain sourdough baguette, toasted (see tips)

50 g (1³/4 oz) soft goat's cheese

30 g (1 oz/¹/4 cup) walnuts, lightly toasted and coarsely chopped

Preheat a chargrill pan or barbecue to high heat. Brush the asparagus with 1 teaspoon of the olive oil and cook for 1–2 minutes each side or until lightly charred and just tender. Set aside to cool slightly.

Combine the asparagus, figs, prosciutto, watercress and chives in a large bowl. Whisk together the remaining olive oil, vinegar and shallot, add to the salad and toss gently.

Spread the toasts with the goat's cheese. Sprinkle the salad and toasts with toasted walnuts and serve.

✦ TIPS ✦

Fresh figs have a short season in late summer and early autumn. When they're out of season, substitute another fresh fruit, such as thin wedges of pear or apple.

This recipe is gluten free if you use gluten-free bread.

NECTARINE, CHICKEN, MOZZARELLA AND MINT SALAD

Fresh nectarines add a delicious sweetness to this light summer salad, but peaches or plums would also work well. Nectarines are high in potassium, which assists electrolyte balance, and their skins are rich in insoluble fibre, so don't peel them. You can serve the grilled chicken warm or at room temperature.

Preparation time: 15 minutes,
    plus 1 hour marinating
Cooking time: 5 minutes
Serves 4

2 tablespoons lemon juice

1 1/2 tablespoons olive oil

1 garlic clove, crushed

500 g (1 lb 2 oz) chicken tenderloins

1 tablespoon mirin

2 teaspoons rice vinegar

1 long red chilli, seeded and finely chopped

400 g (14 oz) can cannellini beans, rinsed

2 nectarines, sliced (see tip)

1 Lebanese (short) cucumber, sliced

50 g (1 3/4 oz/1 cup) baby English spinach leaves

50 g (1 3/4 oz) soft lettuce leaves, such as oak lettuce or butter lettuce

1/2 cup mint leaves

2 tablespoons natural almonds, chopped

1 buffalo mozzarella, drained and coarsely torn

Combine 1 tablespoon of the lemon juice, 1 tablespoon of the olive oil and the garlic in a non-metallic dish. Add the chicken and turn to coat. Cover and refrigerate for 1 hour to marinate.

Heat a chargrill pan over medium–high heat. Drain the chicken and cook for 2–3 minutes each side or until cooked through.

Meanwhile, whisk together the remaining lemon juice, remaining olive oil, mirin, vinegar and chilli to make a dressing.

Combine the cannellini beans, nectarine, cucumber, spinach, lettuce, mint and almonds in a large bowl. Add the chicken, dressing and mozzarella and toss gently before serving.

+ TIP +

You can use peaches, plums or vine-ripened tomatoes in place of the nectarines.

GRANITA
OF PASSIONFRUIT AND MANGO

A granita is the perfect light and refreshing summer dessert.

Preparation time: 10 minutes, plus 4 hours freezing
Cooking time: 5 minutes
Serves 4–6

2 tablespoons raw (demerara) sugar

3 mangoes, coarsely chopped

2 teaspoons lime juice

185 g (6$^{1/2}$ oz/$^{3/4}$ cup) strained passionfruit pulp (see tip), plus extra to serve

Place a large slab tin in the freezer for 2–3 hours. Meanwhile, combine the sugar and 250 ml (9 fl oz/ 1 cup) water in a saucepan over medium heat. Stir until the sugar dissolves; leave to cool completely.

Process the sugar syrup, mango and lime juice in a food processor until smooth. Add the passionfruit pulp and pulse until well combined.

Pour the mixture into the chilled tin (handle it with a tea towel to avoid freezer burn). Cover and freeze for 2 hours or until frozen around the edges. Using a fork, scrape the mixture into icy granules. Freeze for another 2 hours, scraping every 30 minutes.

Serve in chilled glasses, topped with extra passionfruit pulp.

+ TIPS +
You will need about 6 passionfruit for the granita, plus extra to serve.

SALSA
OF WATERMELON, CHILLI AND CUCUMBER

This salsa makes a delicious fresh, healthy accompaniment to grilled fish or chicken, perfect for summer barbecues.

Preparation time: 10 minutes
Cooking time: None
Serves 4 as an accompaniment

300 g (10$^{1/2}$ oz) seedless watermelon flesh, diced (see tip)

1 Lebanese (short) cucumber, diced

4 spring onions (scallions), thinly sliced

2 tablespoons chopped mint

2 teaspoons rice vinegar

2 teaspoons lime juice

1 long red chilli, seeded and finely chopped

Combine the watermelon, cucumber, spring onions and mint in a bowl. Whisk together the vinegar, lime juice and chilli and toss gently with the salsa. Season with sea salt and serve.

+ TIP +
You will need about 400 g (14 oz) watermelon with the rind on to yield 300 g (10$^{1/2}$ oz) flesh.

POACHED PEARS WITH ORANGE, STAR ANISE AND VANILLA RICOTTA
(see recipe page 211)

BAKED PLUMS WITH ALMONDS AND BUCKWHEAT
(see recipe page 210)

BAKED PLUMS
WITH ALMONDS AND BUCKWHEAT

In this healthy, gluten-free twist on a traditional fruit crumble, fresh plums are topped with a crunchy mixture of almonds and buckwheat.

Preparation time: 10 minutes
Cooking time: 20 minutes
Serves 4

6 firm ripe plums (about 500 g/
1 lb 2 oz), halved (see tips)

2 tablespoons almond meal

1 tablespoon chilled butter
or coconut oil

25 g (1 oz/1/4 cup) flaked almonds

2 tablespoons buckwheat kernels

1 tablespoon coconut sugar
or brown sugar

1 teaspoon ground cinnamon

Preheat the oven to 180°C (350°F). Place the plums in a large roasting tin, cut side up (see tips).

Place the almond meal in a bowl. Using your fingertips, rub in the butter until the mixture resembles breadcrumbs. Add the remaining ingredients and stir until well combined.

Sprinkle the crumble over the plums. Bake for 15–20 minutes or until the plums are soft and the crumble is golden brown.

+ TIPS +

You can replace the plums with another type of stone fruit – nectarines, peaches and apricots all work well.

Lining the tin with baking paper makes washing up easier, but it's not essential.

(pictured page 208)

POACHED PEARS
WITH ORANGE, STAR ANISE AND VANILLA RICOTTA

Poached pears make an easy, healthy dessert, especially if you keep the added sugar to a minimum. They're rich in soluble and insoluble fibre and a good source of vitamin C. Serve them with ricotta combined with natural yoghurt for a healthy, deliciously creamy alternative to cream or ice cream.

Preparation time: 10 minutes
Cooking time: 30 minutes
Serves 4

115 g (4 oz/1/3 cup) honey

Juice and thinly peeled zest of 2 oranges

3 star anise

4 firm ripe pears, halved and cored

95 g (3 1/4 oz/1/3 cup) Greek-style yoghurt

80 g (2 3/4 oz/1/3 cup) ricotta cheese

1/2 teaspoon natural vanilla extract

Combine the honey, orange juice, orange zest, star anise and 500 ml (17 fl oz/2 cups) water in a saucepan over medium heat and stir until the sugar dissolves. Bring to the boil, then reduce the heat to low and simmer for 5 minutes.

Add the pears, cover them closely with a piece of baking paper and poach for 15–20 minutes or until tender (the timing will depend on the ripeness of the pears). Remove the pears with a slotted spoon and set aside. Simmer the syrup until reduced by half.

Meanwhile, stir together the yoghurt, ricotta and vanilla.

To serve, spoon the pears into bowls, drizzle with a little syrup and top with a dollop of vanilla ricotta.

✦ TIP ✦

The pears and syrup will keep in an airtight container in the refrigerator for up to 3 days. They're delicious served warm or cold.

(pictured page 209)

BANANA AND BERRY
SPELT BREAD

(see recipe page 214)

**STRAWBERRY, CHIA
AND GINGER JAM**

(see recipe page 215)

BANANA AND BERRY SPELT BREAD

This moist banana bread is sweetened by the natural sugars found in bananas and blueberries, as well as a little honey. Choose pure floral honey for a low-GI option. Blueberries get their vivid blue colour from anthocyanin pigments, phytonutrients with powerful antioxidant and anti-inflammatory effects.

Preparation time: 15 minutes
Cooking time: 55 minutes
Makes 12 slices

Olive oil spray

190 g (6³/₄ oz/1¹/₄ cups) wholegrain spelt flour

2 teaspoons ground cinnamon

1¹/₂ teaspoons bicarbonate of soda (baking soda)

50 g (1³/₄ oz/¹/₂ cup) rolled (porridge) oats

100 g (3¹/₂ oz) fresh or frozen blueberries

300 g (10¹/₂ oz/1¹/₄ cups) mashed ripe banana (see tips)

3 eggs

90 g (3¹/₄ oz/¹/₄ cup) pure floral honey or maple syrup

60 ml (2 fl oz/¹/₄ cup) macadamia oil

1 teaspoon natural vanilla extract

Preheat the oven to 180°C (350°F). Lightly spray a 10 x 20 cm (4 x 8 inch) non-stick loaf (bar) tin with oil. Line the base and long sides with baking paper, extending over the sides.

Sift the flour, cinnamon and bicarbonate of soda into a large bowl. Stir in the oats and blueberries (see tips). Make a well in the centre.

Stir together the mashed banana, eggs, honey, oil and vanilla and pour into the well in the flour mixture. Fold in until just combined.

Spoon the mixture into the tin and smooth the surface with the back of a spoon. Bake for 55 minutes or until a skewer inserted into the centre comes out clean (if it browns too quickly, cover the top with foil). Set aside in the tin for 5 minutes, then turn out onto a wire rack to cool.

✦ TIPS ✦

You will need about 3 bananas for 300 g (10¹/₂ oz) mashed banana.

Stirring the blueberries into the dry ingredients prevents them from sinking during baking.

This loaf can be stored in an airtight container for up to 3 days, or frozen for up to 1 month. Wrap individual slices in plastic to freeze.

(pictured page 212)

STRAWBERRY, CHIA AND GINGER JAM

Try this jam when strawberries are in season, when they're abundant and inexpensive.
Don't worry if the fruit is slightly overripe or damaged – it will be fine for this recipe.
Chia seeds thicken the jam and add extra fibre, while honey replaces the usual sugar as
a sweetener. For a vegan version, replace the honey with rice malt syrup.

Preparation time: 10 minutes
Cooking time: 35 minutes
Makes 500 ml (17 fl oz/2 cups)

750 g (1 lb 10 oz/about 5 cups) fresh or frozen strawberries, hulled and sliced (see tips)

175 g (6 oz/1/2 cup) honey

1 1/2 tablespoons lemon juice

2 teaspoons finely grated ginger

1 teaspoon natural vanilla extract

1 tablespoon chia seeds

Combine the strawberries, honey, lemon juice, ginger and vanilla in a saucepan over medium heat. Bring to a simmer and cook, stirring occasionally, for 30–35 minutes or until reduced and thickened (see tips). Remove from the heat and stir in the chia seeds.

Transfer immediately to a sterilised jar (see tips), cover, cool and refrigerate. The jam will keep for several weeks.

+ TIPS +

You can use any combination of berries you like – raspberries, blueberries and blackberries all work well.

The jam will continue to thicken off the heat after the chia seeds are added.

To sterilise the jar, simply put it through the hot cycle in a dishwasher. Alternatively, wash and rinse it thoroughly, then heat in the oven at 160°C (315°F) for 20 minutes.

(pictured page 213)

ALMOND, DATE AND CRANBERRY CAKE

Packed with sweet dried fruit, this cake doesn't need any extra sugar. The almond meal and mashed pumpkin keep it moist, eliminating the need for a lot of butter or oil. It's very rich, so just a small piece will leave you feeling satisfied.

Preparation time: 15 minutes
Cooking time: 1 hour 20 minutes
Makes 24 small pieces

150 g (5½ oz) seedless raisins

150 g (5½ oz) sweetened dried cranberries

150 g (5½ oz) pitted dates, chopped

185 ml (6 fl oz/¾ cup) fresh orange juice

200 g (7 oz/2 cups) almond meal

100 g (3½ oz) glacé ginger, chopped

1 teaspoon ground cinnamon

1 teaspoon mixed spice

Finely grated zest of 1 orange

125 g (4½ oz/½ cup) mashed pumpkin (winter squash; see tips)

2 eggs, lightly beaten

2 tablespoons macadamia oil

1 teaspoon natural vanilla extract

Preheat the oven to 160°C (315°F). Grease the base and sides of a 20 cm (8 inch) square cake tin and line with baking paper.

Combine the raisins, cranberries, dates and juice in a saucepan over medium–high heat and bring just to the boil. Set aside to cool.

Combine the almond meal, ginger, cinnamon, mixed spice and zest in a large bowl and make a well in the centre. Mix together the pumpkin, eggs, oil, vanilla and soaked fruit and pour into the well. Stir well.

Spoon into the tin and smooth the surface with the back of a spoon. Bake for 1 hour 15 minutes or until the cake is golden, the top firm and a skewer poked into the centre comes out clean. If it browns too quickly, cover with foil. Cool completely in the tin.

✦ TIP ✦

You'll need about 150 g (5½ oz) peeled raw pumpkin to make ½ cup cooked mashed pumpkin.

Store in an airtight container in a cool dark place for up to 2 weeks.

INDEX

Published in 2016 by Murdoch Books, an imprint of Allen & Unwin.

Murdoch Books Australia
83 Alexander Street
Crows Nest, NSW 2065
Phone: +61 (0)2 8425 0100
murdochbooks.com.au
info@murdochbooks.com.au

Murdoch Books UK
Erico House, 6th Floor
93–99 Upper Richmond Road
Putney, London SW15 2TG
Phone: +44 (0) 20 8785 5995
murdochbooks.co.uk
info@murdochbooks.co.uk

For corporate orders and custom publishing contact Noel Hammond, National Business Development Manager, Murdoch Books Australia.

Publisher: Corinne Roberts
Editorial Manager: Jane Price
Design Manager: Madeleine Kane
Editor: Kerryn Burgess
Designer: Susanne Geppert
Photographer: Julie Renouf
Stylist: Kristine Duran-Thiessen
Illustrator: Dominique Sutton-Miles
Production Manager: Alex Gonzalez

Text © Chrissy Freer 2016
Design © Murdoch Books 2016
Photography © Julie Renouf 2016

ISBN 978 1 74336 596 0   Australia
ISBN 978 1 74336 597 7 UK

A cataloguing-in-publication entry is available from the catalogue of the National Library of Australia at nla.gov.au.
A catalogue record for this book is available from the British Library.

Colour reproduction by Splitting Image Colour Studio Pty Ltd, Clayton, Victoria, Australia.
Printed by 1010 Printing International, China.

MEASURES GUIDE: We have used 20 ml (4 teaspoon) tablespoon measures. If you are using a 15 ml (3 teaspoon) tablespoon, add an extra teaspoon of the ingredient for each tablespoon specified.

OVEN GUIDE: You may find cooking times vary depending on the oven you are using. As a general rule, for fan-forced ovens, set the oven temperature to 20°C (35°F) lower than indicated in the recipe.

The author, publisher and stylist would like to thank Fruitos in Byron Bay and Daley's Gourmet Meats in Ballina for their beautiful produce.

ACKNOWLEDGEMENTS

A book is a very personal labour of love, but it simply cannot happen without the talents and efforts of so many other people, who rarely see the recognition they truly deserve.

Thank you, of course, to Murdoch Books for producing such a beautiful book; and to Corinne Roberts, my publisher, for always believing in me and my work and being such a wonderful source of support throughout the entire process.

Thank you to my editor, Jane Price, for keeping me on track and on time and for your talented editing; and to Kerryn Burgess for whipping my text into shape.

To the design team – Madeleine Kane and Susanne Geppert – thank you for your creativity, your stunning pages and, most importantly, your patience. It was worth it in the end! And a special thank you to Dominique Sutton-Miles for producing the most beautiful illustrations; they really do make the book special.

Thank you to the 'dream team' – photographer Julie Renouf and food stylist Kristine Duran-Thiessen. Words cannot describe how talented you two ladies are, what a pleasure you are to work with, your ability to make food come to life, and your amazing friendship. Thank you from the bottom of my heart. And to Anton and Kristine, thank you for once again welcoming us into your home, the beautiful macadamia farm 'Agnutta' in the Byron hinterland.

Finally, and most importantly, thank you to my family. To my parents, Robert and Jean Freer, thank you for being my rock, always loving and supporting me in whatever I do. This book could not have happened without you. And to Harriet (*aka* the midge), the light in my life – you make everything worthwhile.